D0546040

Get Global!

– A practical guide to integrating the global dimension into the primary curriculum

FALKIRK COUNCIL
LIBRARY SUPPORT
FOR SCHOOLS

edited by Tony Pickford

Trenthham Books
Stoke on Trent, UK and Sterling, USA

Trentham Books Limited
Westview House   22883 Quicksilver Drive
734 London Road   Sterling
Oakhill   VA 20166-2012
Stoke on Trent   USA
Staffordshire
England ST4 5NP

© 2009 Tony Pickford

All rights reserved. No part of this publication may be reproduced
or transmitted in any form or by any means, electronic or mechanical
including photocopying, recording or any information storage or
retrieval system, without prior permission in writing from the publishers.

First published 2009

British Library Cataloguing-in-Publication Data
A catalogue record for this book is available from the British Library

ISBN: 978 1 85856 424 1

Designed and typeset by Trentham Print Design Ltd, Chester and
printed in Great Britain by Hobbs the Printers Ltd, Hampshire.

Contents

Contributors

Unless otherwise indicated, the contributors to this book are all subject specialists in the Faculty of Education and Children's Services at the University of Chester.

Tony Pickford is co-ordinator for the foundation subjects and Religious Education in the primary and early years programmes. He is subject leader for History Education.

Ami Davies is a newly qualified teacher from the University of Chester and is now teaching in Shropshire.

Chandrika Devarakonda is a senior lecturer and teaches on the BA Early Childhood Studies programme. Her teaching and research interests are around global dimension, inclusion, equality and diversity.

Sian Duffty is senior lecturer and subject leader for Music Education.

Wendy Garner is senior lecturer on the primary and early years programmes.

Joanne Hurst recently graduated from the University of Chester as a newly qualified teacher. She is teaching in North Wales and the North West area and has a passion for teaching the humanities and ICT.

Malcolm Glover is Associate Dean of Education and Children's Services. He teaches Primary Mathematics Education on the undergraduate and postgraduate Initial Teacher Training programmes.

Luke Jones is subject leader for Physical Education and has an extensive knowledge of National Curriculum Physical Education and teaches across all primary Physical Education programmes.

Ian McDougall is a school consultant for the Diocese of Chester and was a primary school head teacher for many years. He is a visiting lecturer at the University specialising in art and classroom creativity.

Carole Naylor is a lecturer in Science Education on the primary and early years programmes.

Allan Owens is Professor of Drama Education and National Teaching Fellow in the Faculty of Education and Children's Services and Department of Performing Arts at the University of Chester.

Barbara Pickford works for Cheshire County Council and is team leader of Cheshire, Halton and Warrington Traveller Education Service.

Steven Tones is a joint programme leader and partnership manager.

Jane Weavers is the Science subject leader for the primary and early years programmes.

Ackowledgements

The editor would like to thank

- Heather Swainston and staff at Cheshire Development Education Centre for help and support in developing teaching and learning about the global dimension at University of Chester.

- The Grange Infant School in Runcorn for the pictures of an African village and an African city on the cover of this book.

Introduction

What is the global dimension and why should it inform, influence and enhance the primary school curriculum? Global carries multiple meanings. It describes a three-dimensional spherical shape. It implies the comprehensive and the total. Most significantly for us, it relates to worldwide concerns and phenomena. It carries an implied meaning, however, that goes beyond simply the notion of international affairs: it carries connotations of shared concerns at a more human level. Where an international dimension might explore the relationships between nation states, a global dimension is about people and what they have in common, regardless of their nationality, ethnicity or geographical location.

A global dimension to the curriculum will, therefore, be about making children aware of the needs and interests that they share with others across the world. It will be about equipping them with the skills, knowledge and understandings to grapple with complex global issues, as children and in adult life. Fundamentally, it will be about appreciating the impact that they have on others directly and indirectly, through their actions and attitudes – and the impact that the actions and attitudes of others have on them, locally and globally. But perhaps, a more useful question to ask in relation to a global dimension is not 'what ... ?' but 'why ...?'

In 2004, the DfES document, *Putting the world into world-class education: An international strategy for education, skills and children's services,* identified three goals for 'world-class education'. As part of the first goal – 'equipping our children, young people and adults for life in a global society and work in a global economy' – it set the aim: 'to instil a strong global dimension into the learning experience of all children and young people'. The justifications for this were quite utilitarian in nature: the proliferation of journeys abroad, awareness of other cultures in the UK and preparation for work in a 'global economy' (DfES, 2004).

Despite this utilitarian justification, it would be a mistake to underestimate the significance of this and subsequent documents from the DfES: *Developing the global dimension in the school curriculum* (2005) and *Sustainable Schools for Pupils, Communities and the Environment* (2007). As Hicks (2008) notes, they mark a significant shift in official policy towards what he terms, 'global education'. What began as a field on the fringes of mainstream education in the 1970s is now not just supported, but actively promoted by bodies, such as the Qualifications and Curriculum Authority (QCA), the Welsh Assembly Government and the Education subject Centre of the Higher Education Academy (ESCalate).

Others have defined and justified a global dimension to the curriculum more in terms of its intrinsic value. Oxfam, for example, uses the concept of global citizenship to inform the global dimension. In Education for Global Citizenship: A Guide for Schools (2006), Oxfam defines education for global citizenship as an approach which uses 'a multitude of participatory teaching and learning methodologies' to 'develop critical thinking about complex global issues' and to 'develop and express [children's] values and opinions'. The document justifies a global dimension to the curriculum in three ways:

- ■ It provides the knowledge, understanding, skills and values 'to make a positive contribution, both locally and globally'

- ■ It involves children in their own learning through 'the use of a wide range of active and participatory learning methods'

- ■ It encourages children to 'care about the planet' and to 'develop empathy with, and an active concern for others'

It goes on to identify the knowledge, understandings, skills, values and attitudes underpinning a curriculum for global citizenship.

Clark (1997) justifies a global dimension from quite a different perspective, literally through the eyes of the few who have been able to view our planet as a whole entity. His interest is in the structure of the curriculum and the need to reshape the educational system to meet new challenges in the 21st century. In *Designing and Implementing an Integrated Curriculum*, he cites the comments of astronauts who have seen our planet from a distance, to support his vision of education not for global citizenship, but for the development of 'planetary citizens living co-operatively at peace in a global village'. For Clark, this macro vision of education resonates with the personal visions held by many teachers and can be implemented through co-operative, collaborative learning activities at a classroom level.

Although undoubtedly highly idealistic, he argues that the idea of 'planetary citizens' and the development of attitudes and behaviours to facilitate peaceful co-operation can clearly form the basis for a coherent and purposeful curriculum, based on inter-connected thinking and contextualised learning. His starting points for a curriculum for planetary citizenship are focus questions, which can be explored through subjective, time-related, symbolic and ecosystem contexts, as well as the linked perspectives of subject disciplines. A key question, which children will re-visit throughout their schooling, will be 'How does one live responsibly in the global community?' (see Figure 1) – a question which in many ways sums up the essential purpose of a global dimension to the curriculum.

Whether the justification for inclusion of a global dimension in the primary curriculum is utilitarian or idealistic, the starting point is children and their relationship with the wider world – a relationship which is very different from that which prevailed 20 or 30 years ago. In the early 21st century global forces and issues impact on all aspects of society, including the lives of young children. Sometimes described by the much-debated term, 'globalisation', global forces manifest themselves in many different ways: through worldwide communication technologies, such as the Internet; through economic migration; and through industrial location in developing economies. They impinge

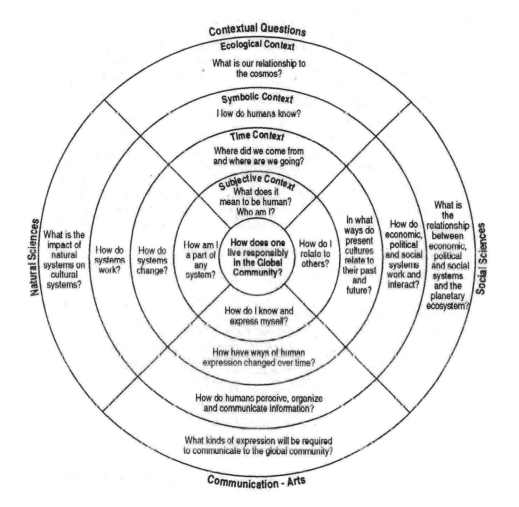

Fig 1. Contextual Matrix with Perspective Questions: 'How Does One Live Responsibly in the Global Community?' – from Clark E (1997) *Designing and Implementing an Integrated Curriculum*. Brandon, Vermont: Holistic Education Press

upon children's lives and experiences through the foods that they eat such as pizzas, curries and southern fried chicken, the clothes that they wear which are invariably manufactured in countries with developing economies and the technologies they use such as television, mobile phones, MP3 players, games and consoles. A BBC survey in 2007 found that over 90 per cent of children in the UK now have access to computers at home and that all children between 6 and 10 years old have played electronic games. More fundamentally, children's friends and relationships are now likely to reflect an increasingly mobile global population: the arrival of families from the EU accession countries since 2004 has greatly increased diversity in areas outside urban centres with long-established multi-ethnic populations. Towns and villages in shire counties in England, with traditionally very low immigrant populations, now have substantial numbers of families from Eastern Europe, greatly increasing the language and cultural experience of hitherto insular communities.

Similarly, global issues are increasingly impacting upon children's lives, especially the issue of climate change. In February 2007, the Inter-governmental Panel on Climate Change reported 'very high confidence that the globally averaged net effect of human activities since 1750 has been one of [global] warming' (IPCC, 2007). This rather innocuous statement confirmed the conclusions of scientists that climate change can only be reversed by the same human action that has created it. How is this relevant to children? The generation now in primary education will probably begin to experience some of the worst effects of climate change when they are adults. Children's lives are increasingly affected by imperatives related to climate change, whether it be the walking bus that takes them to school, more locally-based sourcing of lunchtime food or participation in campaigns to reduce, re-use or recycle waste. Schools now have a clearly defined agenda for sustainability, which should influence not just the management of energy and resources but also the experience of their pupils through everyday routines and curriculum activities.

So what is the global dimension? The DfES publication, *Developing the global dimension in the school curriculum* (2005) identifies eight key concepts:

- Global citizenship
  Gaining the knowledge, skills and understanding of concepts and institutions necessary to become informed, active, responsible citizens

- Conflict resolution
  Understanding the nature of conflicts, their impact on development and why there is a need for their resolution and the promotion of harmony

- Diversity
  Understanding and respecting differences and relating these to our common humanity

- Human rights
  Knowing about human rights including the UN Convention on the Rights of the Child

- Interdependence
  Understanding how people, places, economies and environments are all inextricably interrelated, and that choices and events have repercussions on a global scale

- Social justice
  Understanding the importance of social justice as an element in both sustainable development and the improved welfare of all people

- Sustainable development
  Understanding the need to maintain and improve the quality of life now without damaging the planet for future generations

- Values and perceptions
  Developing a critical evaluation of representations of global issues and an appreciation of the effect these have on people's attitudes and values

The document outlines these concepts and identifies ways in which they can be translated into classroom learning activities and whole school practices and policies. The concepts are valuable in defining the knowledge and skill base of a global curriculum, but are also rather intimidating in their scope and extent. Three key points may help to clarify a way forward in working with and through a global dimension to the curriculum:

- the global dimension is thematic and cross-curricular in nature

- it is concerned with concepts and ideas, which are fundamentally values-based, as well as concerned with skills, knowledge and understanding

- although curriculum-focused, the global dimension has implications for all aspects of school life and experiences.

The global dimension is a cross-curricular theme

The UK National Curriculum is fundamentally based on an analytical, reductionist view of learning, in that it is organised around subjects and areas of learning. Thematic approaches such as the global dimension are not just adjuncts to this model, but can be seen as essentially different, in that they have a basis in a systems approach to learning. Where subject-centred curricula focus on discrete areas of knowledge and sets of cognitive tools, systems-based approaches centre on integrative principles and the inter-connectedness of thinking and learning. How can subject-based planning and case studies, such as those provided by *Developing the global dimension in the school curriculum* (DfES, 2005) or this book, provide support for thematic learning?

Taking an analogy from another DfES document, *Sustainable Schools for Pupils, Communities and the Environment* (2007), subjects can provide doorways into the development of a global curriculum. Like the sustainable schools initiative, the global dimension demands innovation and action across the curriculum and a wide range of school policies. Instead of attempting to change and develop everything all at once,

Sustainable Schools for Pupils, Communities and the Environment suggests that schools start by identifying one or two doorways to sustainability, which can be addressed in a meaningful and manageable way. Similarly, subject contexts provide manageable doorways through which global themes can be addressed. For some schools the humanities may be the first areas of learning to be informed by global issues. For other schools, the doorway of language and literacy may provide a more relevant starting point, through an exploration of stories from a range of cultures or the origins of everyday words. This book is intended as a guide to approaches, activities and ideas you may use, once you have opened the doors to the global dimension offered by a range of curriculum subjects. It is also useful to note that doorways can operate in more than one direction: as well as providing access to global themes, subjects are themselves informed and enhanced by global perspectives.

The global dimension is concerned with concepts and ideas, which are fundamentally values-based, as well as concerned with skills, knowledge and understandings.

The notion that teaching is about imparting values and attitudes, alongside knowledge and understanding, is not new or revolutionary, but in the context of the global dimension, it is far from uncontroversial. Writing on the *Campaign for Real Education* Web site, Standish (2004) criticises the 'new agenda of global civic responsibility' that has 'gained prominence in the geography school curriculum for England and Wales in the 1990s'. He argues that this new agenda

> ... presumes that young people are not capable of maturing into independent political subjects who can reach their own conclusions about social and political issues. Instead of providing them with knowledge to enable them to make their own judgments, geography [or rather a geography curriculum informed by the global dimension] seeks to instil in pupils a set of sociopolitical values it presents as universal. (Standish, 2004)

He goes on to state that 'not only does [the] new agenda inhibit intellectual thought, it is also anti-democratic and intrusive into the private lives of children.'

Though undoubtedly heartfelt, Standish's arguments show a lack of understanding of the so-called new agenda, of which the global dimension is a very significant part, in that he perceives it as being unconcerned with knowledge and understandings. One needs only to glance through DfES (now, Department for Children, Schools and Families) documents, such as *Developing the Global Dimension in the school curriculum* (2005) or similar documents from NGOs, such as Oxfam, to see that the global dimension is heavy with knowledge-based content; in fact, the amount of subject knowledge required may be a key factor in undermining teachers' confidence in the area. His view also fails to recognise that fostering positive values and attitudes has been a key part of teaching and learning in primary schools for many years and is not a pernicious new invention. The Hadow Report of 1931 declared:

> In addition to the ordinary instruction in the various branches of the primary school course, there are other highly important aspects of education for which provision should be made. Every opportunity should be taken, whether in the ordinary lessons or by means of short talks, to inculcate good manners, courtesy and consideration for others, and to develop in the children self-reliance, self-control, thrift, punctuality, kindness to animals and fair play. (*The Hadow Report: The Primary School*, 1931)

The global dimension translates Hadow's 'highly important aspects of education' into concepts applicable to the 21st century and a global society – fostering children's concerns for social justice on a global scale is no different to promoting 'consideration for others' and 'fair play' in the classrooms of the thirties.

Where Standish's argument does have some validity is in his recognition of the tensions and contradictions inherent in teaching about global issues. He maintains that

> ... all pupils today are given the impression that the natural environment is a fragile entity that is being harmed by human actions leaving them with a

pervasive sense of limits. Such an approach fails to deal with the complexities of environmental management and gives the impression that the environment needs to be protected even at the expense of meeting basic human needs. (Standish 2004)

What Standish recognises here is the danger of presenting global issues simplistically, as if there are all-encompassing solutions to essentially simple problems.

Issues of development, for example, are fraught with complexities. In a recent teacher training workshop about climate change, the issue of food miles – a term which refers to the distance food travels from the time of its production until it reaches the consumer – was raised by the trainer. Purchasing food that has been produced in distant countries was characterised as a 'bad thing' in terms of its carbon footprint, leading some participants to resolve that they would cease to buy foods produced in some developing economies. The trainer failed to point out that such actions may address the food miles issue, but could lead to disastrous consequences in less economically developed countries, where farmers may have invested heavily to provide food for supermarkets in the developed world. If large numbers of people boycott their products, farmers would be returned to poverty and reliance on aid. Perhaps the trainer could have made the point that food miles are a significant measure of environmental impact, but that transport is not the only component of food production, which has a carbon footprint. It may be more energy-efficient to produce food in the warmer climates of most developing countries and then transport it to the UK than to attempt to produce food like tomatoes in heated greenhouses.

Similarly, issues in relation to renewable energy are not simple and straightforward. Wind farms and tidal barrage schemes may have the potential to greatly reduce carbon emissions, but they also have a significant environmental impact. Teachers should be wary of presenting them as simple, uncontroversial solutions to the problem of climate change. With older children, it would be appropriate to allow them to research all points of view on a particular renewable energy scheme and debate the pros and cons in an informed manner. Not only would children gain knowledge and understanding in a meaningful context, but they would also develop some insight into democratic processes.

Although curriculum-focused, the global dimension has implications for all aspects of school life and experiences. A global dimension to the curriculum cannot operate in a vacuum and the approaches, values and attitudes implicit within it must permeate all aspects of school life. A global curriculum implies a global school ethos – one that values children's contributions; operates systems of rewards and sanctions that are fair and transparent; aspires to sustainable practices in relation to transport, energy and waste and genuinely respects diversity, whilst celebrating shared values. A global school also has a clear rationale for collaborative and co-operative learning, based on social constructivist principles that are cognitively flexible: learning will build on children's perceptions and starting points, visiting and re-visiting key concepts and ideas with increasing complexity in different contexts and situations.

A global school is inclusive in the broadest sense, and aware of the pitfalls and problems inherent in simplistic approaches. Celebrating cultural diversity is a fundamental part of the curriculum, with an awareness that many different lifestyles and cultures are part of the school community. An understanding and tolerance of diverse cultures is relevant to all children in all schools, regardless of the presence or absence of particular cultural heritages in a given locality. Cultures and heritages which are not obviously present in a school should be respected and included in children's experiences in a way that avoids the development of a sense of otherness. As many schools have discovered since the expansion of the EU in 2004, a school's population can change almost overnight and children who have been taught to perceive diverse cultures as part of their community, not as other cultures in other places, will accept and welcome new arrivals more readily.

In conclusion, a couple of points about the scope and intentions of this book. *Get Global!* is not a definitive and all encompassing guide to implementing the global dimension in primary schools and early years settings. The following chapters do not offer advice in every curriculum subject. There is no separate section on the contribution of Information and Communication Technology (ICT) to global teaching and learning: instead ICT permeates all the subject sections and planning for the development of ICT capability in a global context is implicit, rather than explicit in the activity ideas. Secondly, the ideas and activities that follow are intended as starting points for further development and exploration in the context of your school, not recipes for lessons that guarantee success in any context. The intention is to avoid obvious and familiar approaches. By drawing on the expertise of subject specialists and practicing teachers, you will find new perspectives and fresh approaches to bringing the global perspective into your school.

Finally, a debt must be acknowledged to one of the first and most seminal works in the area of global teaching and learning: Fisher and Hicks's *World Studies 8-13*, published in 1985. With its practical guidance underpinned by theoretical understandings, it has inspired many teachers and had a long lasting impact. *Get Global!* is not a successor or replacement, but a modest attempt to guide and inspire in the same way, with a focus on the foundation stage and the primary age range.

References

Clark, E (1997) *Designing and Implementing an Integrated Curriculum*. Brandon, Vermont: Holistic Education Press.

DfES (2004) *Putting the world into world-class education: An international strategy for education, skills and children's services*. London: DfES.

DfES (2005) *Developing the global dimension in the school curriculum*. London: DfES.

DfES (2007) *Sustainable Schools for Pupils, Communities and the Environment*. London: DfES.

Fisher, S. and Hicks, D. (1985) *World Studies 8-13*. Edinburgh: Oliver and Boyd

Hadow, W.H. (1931) *The Hadow Report: The Primary School*. London: HMSO.

Hicks, D (2008) Ways of Seeing: The origins of global education in the UK. In UK ITE network, *Education for Sustainable Development/Global Citizenship Inaugural Conference*. London 10 July 2008. Bath: Bath Spa University.

IPCC (2007) *Summary for Policymakers: Climate Change 2007 Fourth Assessment Report of the Intergovernmental Panel on Climate Change*. Cambridge and New York: Cambridge University Press.

Oxfam (2006) *Education for Global Citizenship: A Guide for Schools*. Oxford: Oxfam.

Standish A (2004) Geography's New Agenda. In the *Campaign for Real Education* Web site. www.cre.org.uk/geography.html

Chapter 2

Planning for the global dimension

The subject-based and thematically focused sections of this book provide doorways into a global dimension to the curriculum. They indicate ways in which skills, concepts, issues and understanding can be explored from a range of starting points. The starting points you choose will depend on the circumstances of your school; this book does not attempt to define or promote a one size fits all approach to planning for the global dimension. However, there are some key points that are worthy of note whatever your circumstances.

The conceptual framework for a global dimension offered by *Developing the global dimension in the school curriculum* (DfES, 2005) is broad: it ranges across knowledge, skills, understandings, attitudes and values that are quite intimidating in their extent and scope. It does not define a hierarchy of concepts, but states that they 'are all important and interrelated but, in different contexts, different concepts take a more central position and underpin the others' (DfES, 2005). Whilst understandable, this approach is less than helpful in the context of curriculum planning in foundation stage settings and primary schools. Which concepts relate to which contexts? How do the concepts interrelate and underpin each other in different contexts?

At the risk of an over-simplistic analysis, there are concepts within the framework which tend to underpin others in most contexts encountered in the foundation stage and primary years. These concepts form the basis of skills, knowledge and understanding through which more sophisticated ideas within the framework can be explored. These concepts are:

■ *Interdependence*
Fundamental to the global dimension in all contexts, this relates to global connections at a human level as well as the interconnectedness of a global society. It can be developed through the study of contrasting localities in geography, for example, providing children are made aware of the mutually beneficial relationships between more and less developed economies: this should not be a one-way traffic of aid and charitable giving, but a two-way process in which food and raw materials are provided by less economically developed countries, often on exploitative terms. The issue of fair trade – which is a key aspect of social justice – can only be understood through the lens of Interdependence.

■ *Diversity*
Respecting diverse cultures and appreciating biodiversity are fundamental aspects of the global dimension. But a superficial, scattergun approach to diverse cultures will be counter-productive, leading to over-simplification and the reinforcing of stereotypes. In the context of Religious Education, for example, there should be opportunities for in-depth studies of other faiths and traditions, leading to an appreciation of their distinctiveness and a growing understanding of shared beliefs and values.

■ *Global Citizenship (of which knowledge of Human Rights is part)*
This is both a concept within the framework and an overarching theme: it encapsulates the connections between the local and the global through institutions, the media and democratic processes. Children will begin to appreciate how decisions are made and consider their implications through participatory processes and activities within the Citizenship curriculum. For example, a decision to begin a recycling scheme in school has an effect at local level in addressing a wider global issue. At a human level it may provide a connection between children who are recycling and others who have the task of sorting recycled waste in Bangladesh or China.

■ *Sustainable Development*
The finite nature of resources and their sustainable management is a concept often explored through the Science curriculum. Sustainable solutions can be modelled in the virtual world of ICT and in the real world through designing and making activities. Studies of contrasting localities should emphasise that sustainable approaches to development in different places may have different characteristics, due to inequalities and available technology.

Higher order concepts of *social justice* and *conflict resolution*, as well as the critical evaluation of *values and perceptions*, can only be developed by reference to these underpinning concepts in most cases.

The interrelationship of these ideas in the context of subject-based learning is best illustrated through an example of planning. In foundation stage and Key Stage One, stories often provide an appropriate starting point for learning across a range of curriculum contexts. A story, which provides good scope for development of concepts of the global dimension, is *The World Came to My Place Today* by Jo Readman and Ley Honor Roberts, a picture book published by Eden Project Books (2002). It tells the story of George, a young boy who is forced to stay at home because his sister has developed a rash. His grandfather tells him that, instead of going out, the world will come to him for the day. George appears sceptical initially, but is soon impressed by Grandpa's accounts of where everyday materials come from. The global links of daily events – from the arrival of the post to lunchtime to bath time – are illustrated by reference to plant-based products and materials from around the world. Places of origin are identified on a simple pictorial map alongside forms of transport, including boats, ships, aircraft and lorries. Global links range from sources of food – chocolate made from cocoa beans grown in west Africa and sunflower oil from Russia – to sources of household objects – a doormat made from the 'hairy coats of coconuts' in India and towels made using cotton from the southern states of the USA. The visual style of the book is attractive and stimulating; with a mix of cartoon-style illustrations and clear photographic imagery of products and the plants from which they are produced.

The story has potential for subject-based learning across a range of curriculum areas, including literacy, geography and science. This may be the most appropriate starting point for planning and Figure 2 (overleaf) illustrates some subject-based objectives, derived from the National Curriculum programmes of study and the Primary Framework for literacy. Figure 2 also illustrates how these objectives feed into and link to the conceptual framework of the global dimension, as outlined by *Developing the Global Dimension in the school curriculum* (DfES 2005). The arrangement of the concepts from bottom to top indicates an appropriate hierarchy of ideas for Key Stage One. Location of each concept in a separate box is not intended to indicate its isolation: in this context, the concepts in the *Global Citizenship, Interdependence* and *Sustainable Development* boxes are clearly closely linked, if not part of one big idea.

Figure 3 (overleaf) shows the next stage of planning, with subject-based objectives and concepts translated into activities. The cross-curricularity of the global dimension means that the activities within subject and concept boxes are interchangeable. Activities linked to subject objectives are as likely to develop global concepts as those specifically identified as global. Similarly, most activities linked to global concepts will also enhance subject learning – because of the context, most of the examples in the global concept boxes are closely linked to geographical knowledge about sustainability, trade and interconnections.

Based on DfES (2005) *Developing the global dimension in the school curriculum* DfES

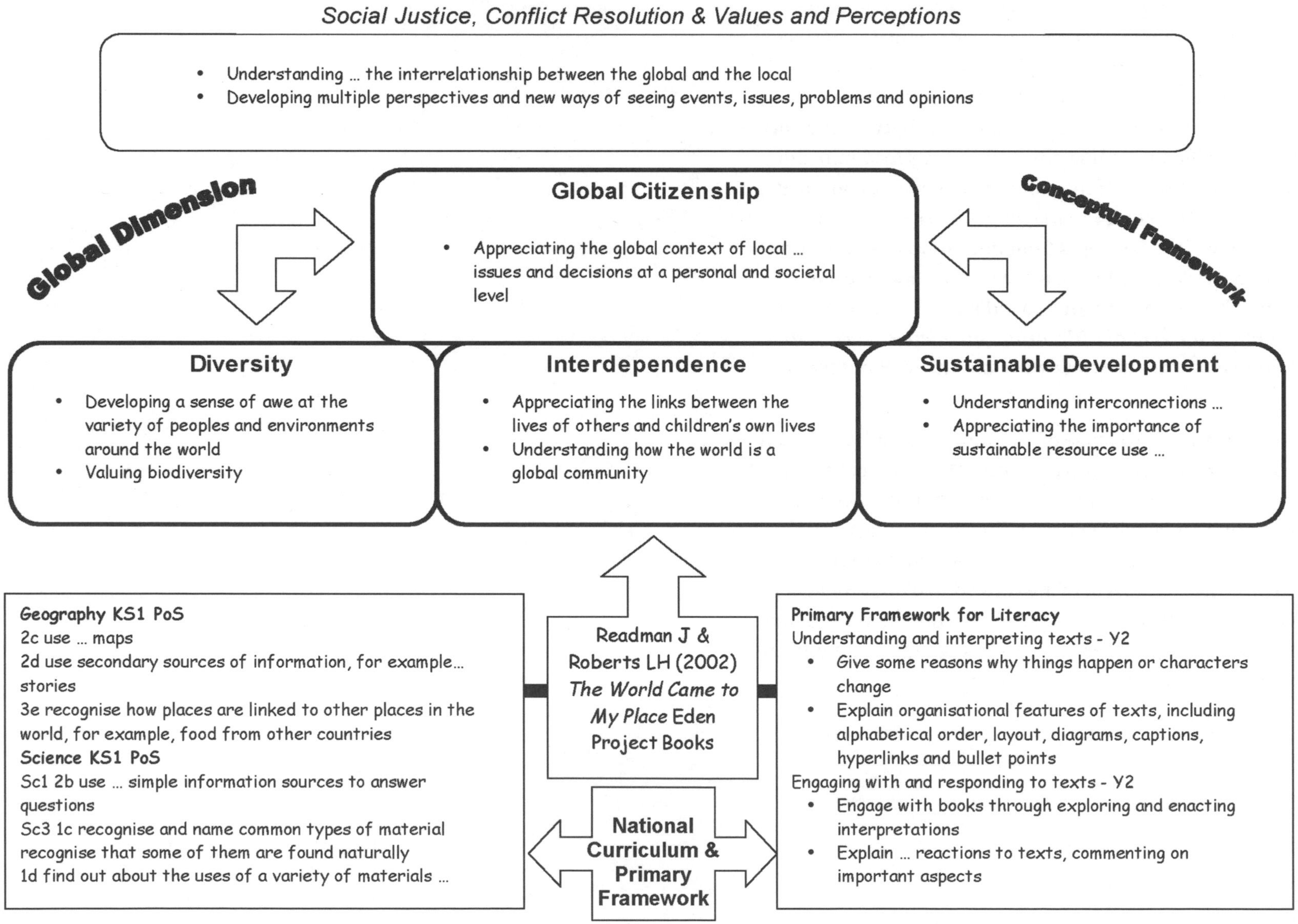

Social Justice, Conflict Resolution & Values and Perceptions

- Understanding ... the interrelationship between the global and the local
- Developing multiple perspectives and new ways of seeing events, issues, problems and opinions

Global Dimension

Conceptual Framework

Global Citizenship

- Appreciating the global context of local ... issues and decisions at a personal and societal level

Diversity

- Developing a sense of awe at the variety of peoples and environments around the world
- Valuing biodiversity

Interdependence

- Appreciating the links between the lives of others and children's own lives
- Understanding how the world is a global community

Sustainable Development

- Understanding interconnections ...
- Appreciating the importance of sustainable resource use ...

Geography KS1 PoS
2c use ... maps
2d use secondary sources of information, for example... stories
3e recognise how places are linked to other places in the world, for example, food from other countries
Science KS1 PoS
Sc1 2b use ... simple information sources to answer questions
Sc3 1c recognise and name common types of material recognise that some of them are found naturally
1d find out about the uses of a variety of materials ...

Readman J & Roberts LH (2002) *The World Came to My Place* Eden Project Books

National Curriculum & Primary Framework

Primary Framework for Literacy
Understanding and interpreting texts - Y2
- Give some reasons why things happen or characters change
- Explain organisational features of texts, including alphabetical order, layout, diagrams, captions, hyperlinks and bullet points
Engaging with and responding to texts - Y2
- Engage with books through exploring and enacting interpretations
- Explain ... reactions to texts, commenting on important aspects

Figure 2: Subjects and the global dimension

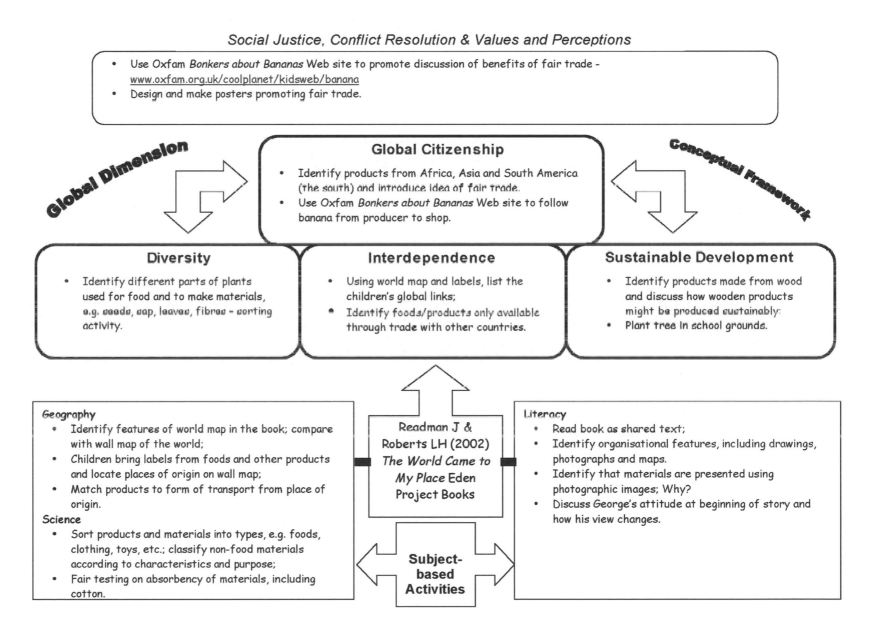

Social Justice, Conflict Resolution & Values and Perceptions

- Use Oxfam *Bonkers about Bananas* Web site to promote discussion of benefits of fair trade - www.oxfam.org.uk/coolplanet/kidsweb/banana
- Design and make posters promoting fair trade.

Global Dimension

Conceptual Framework

Global Citizenship
- Identify products from Africa, Asia and South America (the south) and introduce idea of fair trade.
- Use Oxfam *Bonkers about Bananas* Web site to follow banana from producer to shop.

Diversity
- Identify different parts of plants used for food and to make materials, e.g. seeds, sap, leaves, fibres - sorting activity.

Interdependence
- Using world map and labels, list the children's global links;
- Identify foods/products only available through trade with other countries.

Sustainable Development
- Identify products made from wood and discuss how wooden products might be produced sustainably;
- Plant tree in school grounds.

Geography
- Identify features of world map in the book; compare with wall map of the world;
- Children bring labels from foods and other products and locate places of origin on wall map;
- Match products to form of transport from place of origin.

Science
- Sort products and materials into types, e.g. foods, clothing, toys, etc.; classify non-food materials according to characteristics and purpose;
- Fair testing on absorbency of materials, including cotton.

Readman J & Roberts LH (2002) *The World Came to My Place* Eden Project Books

Literacy
- Read book as shared text;
- Identify organisational features, including drawings, photographs and maps.
- Identify that materials are presented using photographic images; Why?
- Discuss George's attitude at beginning of story and how his view changes.

Subject-based Activities

Figure 3: Activities

13

Chapter 3

English and the global dimension

Jaki Brien

Foundation Stage and Key Stage One: Africa in Fiction

Rationale

The activities described below focus on the theme of Africa because many schools already use the charming picture story book, *Handa's Surprise*, as part of their literacy teaching in Key Stage One. The ideas should augment the work already being undertaken through the inclusion of factual material, realistic characters in contemporary urban settings, and traditional stories. These are chosen to enable children to gain insights about lives which may have superficial differences from their own but also have many similarities. The central concerns of any society are shown in the themes of the traditional stories which pass through generations. The traditional stories are about human relationships and survival in a sometimes difficult environment, so they have clear links with broadening children's perspectives to consider global issues. There is also a text which can hardly be categorised as fiction because it focuses on making direct, factual links between the contrasting lives of a child in America and a Masai girl. Finally, for children approaching the end of Key Stage One, a challenging and mind-expanding poem by James Berry is included. Not many children will be ready for it and many teachers may fight shy of it but for those classes who work with it, *Fantasy of an African Boy* is a profoundly valuable text.

No specific objectives from the renewed Primary Framework for Literacy and Mathematics are stipulated for the following activities. However, when planning, the activities can be adapted or extended to produce the objectives necessary for different year groups to fit in with a school's planning cycle. To make this clearer the standard unit headings and suggested age groups are included as a title for each activity. Niki Daly would be an excellent choice for the Y2 unit on Significant Authors.

Foundation Stage
Books

Daly, Niki (2006) *Not so fast, Songololo*. **London: Francis Lincoln Children's Books**

> **Story synopsis**: Shepherd lives on the outskirts of an unidentified city in South Africa. He has very old trainers (*takkies*) On a trip to the city with his grandmother, he sees bright red *takkies* which his grandmother buys for him.

Daly, Niki (2006) *Happy Birthday, Jamela*. **London: Francis Lincoln Children's Books**

> **Story synopsis**: Jamela is disappointed when her mother buys her sensible school shoes instead of the pretty 'princess' shoes which she really wanted so she glues glitter and sparkly beads to them to make them pretty for her birthday party. Her mother isn't pleased! Jamela's neighbour Lily likes the shoes so they decorate more shoes and sell them on the market, making enough money to replace the ruined school shoes and to buy (as a surprise) the 'princess shoes' which she liked so much.

> **Activities focus**: Speaking, Listening and responding (Reception)

As both these books are about shoes, the idea is that we start children thinking about global perspectives with the metaphorical walking in the shoes of others! (It is interesting that *Not so Fast, Songololo,* which was written in 1985, depicts an apartheid South Africa whereas *Happy Birthday, Jamela* (2006) shows an integrated city community.)

The stories offer children the context in which to describe incidents from their own experience. By shaping these as a recount, they will be able to work with tenses and ordering while developing the understanding of the story which they will need as a basis for later writing through extended oral language. While listening and responding to children's recounts, practitioners should focus on both temporal connectives, (first, then, next) and on descriptive language, modelling both these through recounting their own experience of buying shoes.

This aspect of the work can be reinforced through a role play area set up as a shoe shop and through a dance/drama activity where children move as they would wearing imaginary old trainers which are too small, new trainers, school shoes and party shoes. This could also be extended to include other kinds of shoes which are not in the stories.

Practitioners can also build new stores of words through practical D&T activities based on *Jamela's Birthday*. Children thoroughly enjoy sticking glittery bits on old shoes! Practitioners working with them should focus on developing descriptive language, particularly the use of adjectives.

Small world play could be directed to recreating Songololo's journey to town.

The activities above are about children understanding the stories and projecting themselves into the characters in situations which are familiar to them. The more explicitly global aspect of these texts would be seeking the clues in the illustrations and texts which enable us to see the similarities and differences between childhood in Britain and South Africa.

From *Not so Fast, Songololo* we find out:

- the names aren't familiar (*Gogo* for grandmother, *takkies*).
- the currency is different (Rands)
- the weather is hot
- villages don't have traffic lights or pedestrian crossings
- most people travel by bus

Happy Birthday, Jamela tells us:

- Jamela speaks two languages, *Xhosa* and English
- Some Xhosa words and phrases
- Markets are less formal than in Britain.

Young children are fascinated by different languages and really enjoy word play so it would be worth learning to sing *Happy birthday to you* in Xhosa. There would also be many opportunities in a Foundation stage setting to use *Enkosi* – which means thank you. It would also be possible to add to children's store of words by thinking of all the different words we have for footwear. This will encourage children to realise that we choose words to convey exactly the meanings we need.

It's worth looking at the range of words from dialects of English which all mean shoes designed for sports.

From British dialects we have:

- Sandshoes: South West
- Daps. South Coast
- Pumps: North West
- Plimsolls (plimmies): South East
- Gloria Gaynors or Claire Rayners
- Creps: London
- Gutties: Scotland and Northern Ireland

In America they are called sneakers, tennis shoes, gym shoes or running shoes and in Australia they are keds.

This work, brought informally into discussion, teaches the basics of language diversity – that we may have different words but we are usually expressing the same thoughts and feelings.

Year One
Book
Lupton, H (1998) The Blind Man and the Hunter in *Tales of Wisdom and Wonder*. Barefoot Books

> **Story synopsis**: A hunter takes a blind man out into the forest where he is impressed that the blind man 'sees with his ears.' The next day the hunter tries to trick the blind man but later regrets doing so.

> **Activity focus**: Listening and responding, Engaging with and responding to texts, Drama.

The Blind Man and the Hunter is a West African story. Like many traditional stories it is deceptively simple, just a story about a hunter who tries to trick a blind man and comes to regret it. Like all the best stories, it lingers in the mind and grows in scope each time you think about it. It is a brilliant story which turns on the two questions asked by the hunter and the answers given by the blind man.

- 'If you're so clever and you see with your ears, then answer me this: why is there so much anger and hatred and warfare in this world?' And the blind man answered: 'Because the world is full of so many people like you- who take what is not theirs.'

- 'If you're so clever and you see with your ears, then answer me this: Why is there so much love and kindness and gentleness in this world?' And the blind man answered: 'Because the world is full of so many people like you – who learn by their mistakes.'

Traditional stories are usually better learnt by the teacher and told, rather than read. However, this version is ideal for reading aloud, so a rehearsed, careful reading would be fine.

It is best to start the activities in a drama lesson. We want children to enter into the world of the story: at year one, the whole body tends to get involved, not just the mind. Start with the part of the story where the two men are walking through the forest for the first time. The children could be in pairs and would be encouraged to talk about what the hunter is seeing and what the blind man is hearing. The incidents with the lion and elephant could be re-enacted with the contrasting characters being asked to think about how they move and what they think about the situation and about each other. This is the point of the story where the hunter begins to respect the blind man.

Then we move on to the part of the story where the hunter takes the two birds from the traps and decides which one to give to the blind man , who has caught the much better bird. Working individually, the children have to decide why the hunter did as he did. You could then work on developing the story to decide what would happen if the hunter had been more honest.

The rest of the work on this story would be based in the classroom and would address the two huge questions asked by the hunter. Hopefully, for the children we teach, the world is much more 'full of love and kindness and gentleness' than 'anger and hatred and warfare,' so start there, encouraging the children to talk about, write about and depict visually the good things of the world which they know. We would move on to the darker question and think about the things which are wrong in the world. The final oral stage would be to consider whether the blind man was right in his answers. In our own classroom worlds, certainly children (and teachers!) can make the world better if we learn by our mistakes and share the generosity towards the mistakes of others which is shown in this story.

The children could be asked to write the story as a shared activity taking the point of view of one of the characters. The writing possibilities will be very obvious to all teachers but don't do this story to death by overworking it!

Croll, Virginia (1994) *Masai and I.* London: Puffin Books

Story synopsis: An American girl is learning about the *Masai* people in school and thinks about what her life would be like if she were *Masai*.

Activity focus: Understanding and interpreting texts, Creating and shaping texts.

This is an interesting text because it is more than just fiction. The factual material is made very obvious so it is a useful resource for teaching that we can learn from many different sources. The year one objectives in the Primary Framework ask children to learn to distinguish between fact and fiction, so this text would be good to use following more overt examples of recognisable genre. The key features of the text which merit further exploration are in language terms: the use of a present tense; the ways descriptive language is put together and the use of conditional verb forms. In terms of global perspectives, the reader is asked to empathise with a child from a happy, but different, society and consider the merits of different lifestyles. There is always the danger that such comparisons reinforce stereotypes about less economically developed countries; Kroll's text shows the Masai people as admirable.

Read the book through once with the children to understand the story and then come back to it with the specific task of identifying the ways in which the two lives differ. This is made explicit on every page so the children will soon be able to adopt the 'If I were Masai I would . . .' language form. This can also be used to help beginning writers to frame a written response. 'If I were Masai I would like...'. More advanced writers can be asked to include their own extended descriptive language, choosing their verbs and adjectives carefully.

The work could also be developed into simple fold and cut booklets in which children write and illustrate what they have discovered about Masai people; lists comparing the two life styles; lists of words particularly liked in the book to extend the children's stock of words. Also look closely at the book to make the more difficult comparisons between the urban American life lived by Linda in the story and the lives of the children in the class you are teaching. For example, Linda is allowed to play outside until dark and to go to the corner shop with her little brother. Triangles could be made up of sentences or illustrations to show three different sets of expectations for children. It will be interesting to see which the children prefer!

Year Two

Aardema, Verna (1981) *Bringing the Rain to Kapiti Plain.* **MacMillan**

> **Story synopsis:** This is a re-working into verse of a traditional Kenyan folktale. Ki-Pat looks after a herd of cattle on the Kapiti Plain. During a drought, he saves the herd by firing an arrow into a thundercloud to make it rain.

> **Activity Focus:** Speaking, Drama, Understanding and interpreting Texts, Creating and shaping texts.

This book almost sits there begging you to turn it into a class assembly! With this in mind, the suggested activities could each be of real value in isolation or could be brought together to present the work to an audience.

As with all books, the starting point must be working as a class to get the meaning from the text and recognising its special qualities. These are:

- use of rhyme. The rhyme pattern is a bit tricky as the usual ABAB scheme is dropped when the author wants to add emphasis

- use of repeated stanzas which gradually accumulate to give the complete story like *This is the House that Jack built*, upon which it was modelled

- that the rhythm is essential to gain full meaning from the text

- that there are some unfamiliar words

Preliminary activity: Compare the pictures of the cattle before and after the rains fall, making contrasting lists of descriptive vocabulary starting with the senses. Vision is easiest to start with but go on to thinking about what you would expect to hear, smell and touch on the plains in the two pictures. Bring these together to form class list poems.

For example:

Ki-Pat sees:
> Tall, dead grasses
> Yellowing, brown and rusty gold.
> Cows staggering. Cows falling
> Thin and hungry
> Rough tongues lolling
> Eyes dully and gluey
> Ribs like toast racks
> Horns like long white rib bones

Ki-Pat hears:
> Dead grass rustling
> Dead twigs snapping
> Cows calling for sweet water
> Cows calling for fresh grass
> Cows thudding to the ground

Main Activity: If possible take the children out into the playground just after it's rained to help with the second list. Then extend the poems by adding a verse for each situation to show what Ki-Pat feels. List poems are a wonderful genre because, however weak individual lines seem, a bit of careful editing (use an interactive whiteboard for whole class sharing) and re-ordering always makes them really good. With Key Stage One children, the editing process is best described as: **change, add, move, delete** – all of which could be undertaken as shared work or groups of children could be given the original phrases to cut and paste, literally or electronically into final poems.

The second activity involves preparing the poem for a group performance. Have different groups with paintings to hold up at the relevant time but you might prefer to include some mimed actions as well. The children will be able to learn the poem remarkably easily, partly because children are really good at memorising and partly because the poem is 90 per cent repetition. The performance should focus on clarity, rhythm, using the punctuation to convey sense and changing expression to denote the sad and happy parts.

The third activity to develop from this text extends the way in which we view comprehension with young children. In the previous example (*Masai and I*) I suggested ways in which children could be encouraged to draw literal, inferential and appreciative understanding from the text. With *Bringing the Rains to Kapiti Plains* there is huge potential for taking a different approach. The spare story gives little direct information about the Kapiti Plain or about Ki-pat and his life as a herdsman. It does, however, give marvellous opportunities to frame questions based on the text and seek answers. This is an important part of learning to read: realising not only that text tells us interesting stuff but it may also point us to further questions. The enquiring, engaged reader will come away from a text bursting with questions but too often these are stifled by the pace of the curriculum and this important aspect of comprehension is underdeveloped.

As an experiment I decided to find out how long it would take me to answer two questions 'How much rain could have fallen from the thundercloud?' and 'What sort of eagles fly over Kapiti Plains?' These are only two of the many questions which could be derived from the story. Within three days I had informed answers to both; children could easily do the same. This is how I suggest you go about it.

- Discuss the things which the story doesn't tell you and use these to form questions

- Choose a question to work through together

- Pick key words from the question and put them into the Web using a search engine. You may not get a constructive answer to start with – the first attempt to find out about eagles in Kenya gave me a great deal of information about an American University's Football team tour of the country!

- Such failures encourage children to think about grouping and classifying words under broad headings -'eagles' may not get you anywhere but Kenya Wildlife, Nature or Birds will all do so

- You will easily find constructive general sites but probably won't get the information you want. This is where the children we now teach

are more fortunate than any other preceding generation – most good Web sites will give you the opportunity to make contact and nearly everyone in the world is willing to answer children's genuine questions

- The next stage is to compose an appropriately polite email to a complete stranger. This could be as good a bit of shared writing as you will ever undertake as it has a genuine audience, requires a particular genre and therefore grammar and vocabulary and needs to express the question clearly and concisely. I never understand why we spend so much time and effort teaching children how to write letters to fictional characters and so little on the emerging etiquette of email

- Send it and wait for the reply

- Always make the children thank their correspondents for the time and effort put into replying to the questions

To return to my example questions, Shailesh Kumar Patel of *Nature Kenya* told me that both Tawny and Bateleur eagles fly over Kapita Plain and Doug Parker of the Institute of Climate and Atmospheric Science at the University of Leeds wrote:

> If you want to know what it's like inside a cloud, think of a foggy day. Although it can feel quite wet in the fog, you can still breathe the air, and it is nothing like as wet as being underwater. Most of the foggy air is just air, and only about one part in 100,000 of the fog (by volume) is water. The same is true inside a cloud.
>
> If a cloud is black, it means it is blocking out a lot of the sunlight and this means that it is very tall. A big, black cloud may be 10km or 10,000 m from its base to its top. If you squashed all that cloud into a thin layer, that layer would be 0.1 m deep. This would produce a layer of water 0.1m=10cm deep over the ground.
>
> Some thunderstorms in Africa can produce this much rain in a few hours ...

These replies show the learning in terms of global perspectives which can be derived from this activity. If children can learn that the world is full of learned, helpful people, willing to share their knowledge generously, they will certainly have reached a new understanding of the world. To me, it seems just short of miraculous that I can flip through a picture book, frame a question, find an expert anywhere in the world and receive an answer in a few days. I hope that the children share my wonder at this.

If you work through these activities, you will have five minutes performance poetry, the children's own list poems and accounts of the information you have discovered to augment the story. Put this together and you have a good assembly!

Some teachers may like to go further to consider why lack of rainfall has become such a problem in sub-Saharan Africa and what can, and must, be done about it.

Berry, James (1995) Fantasy of an African Boy in Mitchell, A. (ed.) *The Orchard Book of Poems Orchard*

> **Poem synopsis:** An African boy muses about the strangeness of money, saying that it can't be eaten, drunk, read or used as medicine yet without money, people starve, thirst, lack education, and die of curable diseases. He imagines money flying freely throughout the world 'just like dropped leaves in wind!'

> **Activity focus:** engaging with and responding to text.

This is not a poem for the faint-hearted! It is rich, complex and provocative. Handled gently with a mature class, this could lead to really interesting discussion.

Start by reading the poem aloud. It's difficult so you'll need to rehearse it thoroughly. I would not immediately ask for responses to the theme but start by asking the children to imagine who they think James Berry was pretending to be as he composed the poem. Don't accept 'an African boy' as an answer! Go deeper and further by asking questions such as: Is he older than you or younger? 'Is he rich or poor?' 'What do you imagine his life story to be so far?' 'What do you think will happen to him?' 'What sort of person writes a poem like this?'

Next I would focus on a couple of the verses, reminding the children that English is used by people all over the world and that Berry has deliberately made language choices in this poem to distance the reader from the character, while expressing the ideas in new ways.

Take the lines

> Everybody says it's a big,
> bigger brain bother now,
> money ...

Don't ask the children to translate them into conventional English but ask them to say what they mean to them. Explain that poets hope that everyone will make something slightly different out of their work and that their intention is to set off unique trails of thinking in each reader's mind.

Go on to the lines:

> Such walled-round gentlemen
> overseas minding money! Such
> bigtime gentlemen, body guarded
> because of too much respect
> and too many wishes on them

Ask the children how the African boy of the title feels about the people with money. Again, take the information from the words written not from any thoughts about how you would expect people to feel.

Finally, work with the image of money flying everywhere, doing its magic. What would the world be like?

It might be a mistake to try to get written work from this stimulus but money mobiles would be fun. Children could create their own notes (don't photocopy banknotes – it's illegal) and write on them what they would like to free money to do. As this is the sort of poem you'll approach in the summer term, tie the notes to cotton and let them waft from railings or trees in the playground. Doubtless, they will eventually be pulled down but in the meantime other minds may be opened to the children's ideas.

Key Stage Two – Fantasy Worlds in Books without Words
Rationale

For Key Stage Two the activities focus on developing global themes through picture books without any words. These books, which are written for children of this age group, are being published more frequently and certainly represent some of the most interesting approaches to issues in children's literature. They have particular value in encouraging children to consider the impact of visual literacies, linking well with the broad interpretation of text seen in the renewed Primary framework for literacy. Narrative presented without words has other advantages for the teacher as it is accessible for pupils who are new to written English and allows equal access to activities to children who are struggling with reading or lack motivation. Given current concerns about boys' writing, all the texts chosen are 'boy friendly' and for each text at least one writing activity is suggested.

However, these pragmatic reasons are not why texts without words are of particular value. Their unique strength is that they are more open to a range of interpretations than a book which is controlled by a written authorial perspective. Though it would be grossly naïve to suggest that an illustration cannot be biased or persuasive in tone, such bias is more easily interpreted by children and can usefully become a focus for class work. Nikki Gamble (2008) suggests that children's literature can act as a window to the world or as a mirror in which we see ourselves more clearly. Each of the sets of activities below is designed to further each of these perspectives through the exploration of a fantasy situation which can either reflect back to us our own preconceptions about the real world or open insights into a world as yet unknown or explored.

Year 3 and Four
Book
Popov, Nikolai (1998) *Why?* Zurich Switzerland: North-South Books

> **Story synopsis**: A frog is sitting in a field happily smelling a flower but is attacked by a rabbit. The confrontation develops into a war which destroys the field.

> **Activity focus**: Drama, Creating and Shaping texts.

Start by sharing the text, slowly turning the pages and asking children in pairs to whisper their text for the pages to each other. The idea of the whispering is to set a quiet tone for the following activities. Then move onto some work with the teacher in role as the author and the children as interviewers. This book has a really helpful and moving author's note at the end which gives you all the information you need to allow the children to form questions about his life and his motivation for writing this book. Some children in Year three will be able to use the information they have gained from this activity to write a report on Nikolai Popov, others will be ready to attempt to write the report in first person. Children who are new to written English will be able to reinforce reading and writing skills if they are given written prompts to complete sentences or questions to sort according to whether the answer is 'yes' or 'no'.

Having established the narrative and purpose of the text, a second activity would be to explore the perspectives to the story. In the book the frogs are depicted as the goodies so it would be good to look at where a story starts and how this can influence the reader's attitude. Ask the children to work in small groups or pairs to create a scene to insert before Popov's book starts which would change the perspective so that the rabbits appear to be in the right. Make it clear to the class that not even pretend fighting is permissible. These scenes could then be performed for the other children and the actors asked, still in role, to respond to questions in ways which justify their actions. eg 'So, if the rock and the flowers were really yours not Frog's, why did you go away?'

The drama can then be used to frame writing of texts for the book from the perspective of the rabbits or the frogs. Perhaps this would be a good time to introduce the idea that history is always written by the victors. Children are quick to realise that the war destroys the very things that the rabbits and frogs were fighting about in the first place so, as Popov says, it was futile. This could lead to creating an additional scene or page through drama, art and writing which extends the story and shows whether the rabbits and frogs learn from their experiences.

Wiesner, David (2006) *Flotsam*. New York: Houghton Mifflin Books

Story synopsis: A boy is on the beach when an old camera is washed ashore. When he gets the film developed he discovers amazing secrets about life in the oceans and an even stranger secret about the camera itself. (NB a detailed synopsis would spoil the enjoyment of coming to this beautiful book for the first time.)

Activity focus: Speaking, Creating and shaping texts

Don't start by sharing this text with a whole class. It would be better to have the book available for a week or so before working with it to ensure every child has an opportunity to become familiar with the book.

Years three and four are the time when children's vocabulary rockets and they become adept at choosing exactly the words they need to convey ideas or feelings. However, focusing on long pieces of writing often prevents them from searching for the perfect word. For this reason, it is ideal for this age group to explore two short poem forms, the *haiku* and *quinquain* which both ask for well chosen observations but bring different cultural perspectives to poetry.

The haiku is a Japanese form which uses three lines only. The first line has five syllables, the second has seven and the third has five. The idea of haiku is to describe a scene with deceptive simplicity. Strangely, the conventions of the form extend rather than restrain the imagination. The quinquain is a recent American form which seeks to adapt the haiku to English rhythmic patterns by using pairs of stressed and

unstressed syllables. The syllable pattern in 2,4,6,8,2. Please remember to tell the class that they were invented by Adelaide Crapsey as this never fails to amuse children.

Fortuitously, *Flotsam* features both an American boy and a Japanese girl so it sis appropriate to work on creating two mini anthologies which describe the fantasy photographs of the seas: one anthology creating the American quinquains and the other Japanese haiku. Use the usual sequence of shared reading- shared writing- guided writing- independent writing. As the forms will automatically provide writing frames, this is well within the scope of the children.

Here are two models:

Haiku
Beneath fish-lit lamps
Kind and wise, the octopus
Reads to his triplets

Quinquain
Above
The schools of whales
Huge starfish stride the seas
With unimagined countries on
Their backs.

The second activity asks children to see the world from other perspectives. The book includes photographs of all the children from different countries who discovered the secret of the camera before sending it back on its voyage. Let the children choose one of the characters in the book, or the person they imagine will find the camera next and answer this questionnaire as that character, either individually or in pairs.

- What's your name?

- Where do you live?

- Why were you on the beach that day?

■ How were you feeling before you found the camera?

■ What three words best describe your feelings when you first saw the photographs?

■ What was the most amazing image of the sea?

■ Can you describe one of the photographs you saw and kept? (Use your imagination. Draw a picture first if it helps)

■ How has this experience changed you?

■ What's your message for the next person to find this camera?

Any of these answers can be developed into an extended piece of writing if you wish. You could certainly link this work to art. It would also be excellent to link this to ICT by using a digital camera to try to reproduce the effects of photographs within photographs.

Year five and six
Book

Van Allsburg, Chris (1996) *The Mysteries of Harris Burdick.* **Boston Massachusetts: Houghton Mifflin Books** (Try to order the portfolio edition – more expensive but well worth it!)

> **Story synopsis:** There isn't one! There are fourteen (fifteen in the portfolio edition) faintly strange, black and white pictures each with a title and a caption. These purport to be have been left at a publishing house by an author called Harris Burdick, who promised to come back the next day with the stories to go with the pictures but was never seen again.

> **Activity focus:** Group discussion and interaction, Creating and shaping texts, Presentation.

These extraordinary illustrations are a perfect stimulus for the extended writing which needs to be emphasised in upper Key Stage Two. In determining how to use them, the teacher needs to know each child's preferred authorial approach which is probably emerging at this stage. Some prefer to work alone, allowing the pictures to open gates in the imagination; others prefer to collaborate, talk and share ideas. Some make notes; some draft willingly; others prefer to plan and rehearse their writing in their heads. Working with *The Mysteries of Harris Burdick* is a big commitment so it's wise to enable the children to write in their preferred ways.

A starting point for working with these pictures must be character development. An experienced writer knows much more about the characters than ever appears in the text so it is important that young writers are given a frame for character development. This can be as a questionnaire (as in the *Flotsam* activity above) or in role-based activity. The writer should know who is going to be central to the story. This is not just about name and appearance but also interests, likes, beliefs, fears and hopes for themselves and the world. This activity may seem to be about Gamble's 'windows' into understanding of difference but it is also very much a 'mirror' as well; Caryl Phillips suggested that: 'A writer begins by breathing life into his characters. But if you are very lucky, they breathe life into you.' This quotation could be a very useful starting point for discussion.

Once character is established, move on to 'setting.' The places in these stories have a transitory familiarity; they are just a step to the side of the known. Start with asking the children where they have been that is most like the picture before moving on to considering how it is different and how the feelings evoked by this imagined place could be conveyed to a reader.

Once the children know their 'where' and 'who' for the story, the narrative will form quite easily. I would set the stipulation that the caption given by Van Allsburg must be included because this will make the children's writing more ingenious and original.

Following original drafting, encourage sharing of texts in writing conferences. If a class is unfamiliar with this way of working you may need to take on the role of editor. The purpose of editing at this point is to encourage the writer to create more effective text and shaping so that their unique ideas are conveyed to the audience.

There is little point in editing for audience if there is to be no audience. This is another facet of a global perspective enabled by this text. Children's work can be read, shared and published on a dedicated website: www.chrisvanallsburg.com . Here children can enter a global community of those who have responded to *The Mysteries of Harris Burdick*. They will discover that they share ideas and solutions with people of different ages, living very different lives across the world. Hopefully, they will find an empathy with other writers but also a sense of their own uniqueness. No one will choose exactly the same words and phrases or have been taken on the same imaginative journey.

Do one yourself! In all extended writing it is of huge value to be able to speak authoritatively (pun intended) about the activity and the decisions needed. It would be excellent to model each aspect of the writing process to give the children insight into expectations and possibilities.

Tan, Shaun (2006) *The Arrival.* **London: Hodder**

Story synopsis: A man has to leave his wife and child and sail to another country to seek work. On arrival, everything is strange to him; he cannot understand the language or the ways of life. With help he finds food, accommodation and work. He makes friends and learns of the circumstances that drew others to this country. He saves enough money for his wife and daughter to join him. They are happily re-united and at the end of the book, his daughter helps another newcomer begin to find his way in this new land. From reading this synopsis, *The Arrival* could seem dull and possibly unattractive to children. It really isn't. It is a saga of real complexity presented in a wordless form. The many layered story is totally involving and thought-provoking.

Activity focus: Understanding and interpreting texts, Text structure and organisation

The temptation, when considering work based on a book without words, is to plan activities which supply the 'missing text'. This would be a mistake when exploring *The Arrival* with a class. The main point of the book is to consider how, when deprived of the easy solutions offered by our separate languages, we can still draw on the universal languages of facial expression, gesture, gifts, drawings and symbols to communicate. Because of this theme, avoid activities which ask the children to provide unnecessary words for narration. Instead, focus on working to deepen their understanding of the text and writing in ways which extend the story beyond the narrative.

Ask children to consider the first few pages to try to determine what makes the man leave the country of his birth. A threat is depicted as great spiky dragon tails in the sky and streets. The threat seems to be general; the man is one of many who leave on the same day. Later in the the book, he is scared by the spiked tail of another creature – so the threat may be depicted literally. Equally plausibly, the threat may be allegorical; the creatures could represent poverty, intolerance, unemployment or disease. Later in book we see that people leave countries because of invasion, war and forced labour. Children might find it helpful to consider some of the reasons for emigration to help them to conclude what made the man leave. It is important in this activity that they do not feel that there is one right answer. They are exploring a complex area in the safety net of a fantasy setting. If they learn that reasons are seldom simple and that, given the same information other people may reach different solutions, their discussion will be of value and will enhance their reading of this text.

Some children will be intrigued by the amount of script which bombards the man in his new land. They could collect the symbols and their meanings and create a glossary. This could lead to investigation of whether all languages work in the same way as English. Children may have knowledge to share but this shouldn't be demanded by a teacher. While we may wish to celebrate and applaud diversity many children approaching puberty want nothing more than to be exactly like everyone else.

If this is the case it is better to keep within the fantasy world of the book and try to create the rest of the language as a group activity. They will start with a few words, usually nouns, but can be encouraged to think more deeply. For example, if they have identified the symbol for bread, you could ask them what kinds of bread are going to be sold in this world. You will need ways of distinguishing and subdividing. Is this going to be done with adjectives? If so, are they going to be positioned in the same way? If you have a word for blue, will your language enable you to express the idea of bluer? This not only reinforces the terminology of English but also encourages children to recognise that languages may differ in surface features but all arose from the same needs and enable the sharing of universal ideas.

On the end pages of this book there are sixty different portraits of people. Ask each child to choose a person and create an arrival story for that character in the same way that the additional stories within the book are created. Before composing the wordless narrative the children will need to make a lot of decisions such as: what made them leave? What did they pack? What skills did they have? Who and what did they leave behind? How did they escape? How did they pay? How did they travel? What do they miss most? What are their hopes and fears? What do they do in this new land? Have they reached a happy ending? This part of the work might be better undertaken collaboratively: children could work together with a pair of the portraits. When all this information has been assembled, the children will be ready to create their wordless text. This is a writing activity as they will augment the skills of ordering, logical sequencing, omission, creation of tension and inclusion of detail which will enhance future narrative composition.

Chapter 4

Mathematics and the global dimension

Malcolm Glover

Rationale

Although it is not within the scope of this chapter to provide a rationale for teaching mathematics, it is useful to identify what mathematics as a discipline contributes to our thinking in order to set a context. The Cockcroft Report identified the usefulness of the subject in providing '...a means of communication which is powerful, concise and unambiguous' and also identified how mathematics supplies skills for employment and skills to be used in other subjects (Cockcroft, 1982). This view is echoed in the Mathematics section of the National Curriculum document:

> Mathematics equips pupils with a uniquely powerful set of tools to understand and change the world. These tools include logical reasoning, problem-solving skills and the ability to think in abstract ways. (DfES, 1999)

However, it is difficult to see how a child could learn how to use all of these tools in a vacuum and apply them with confidence to the world. It is easier to see how beginning to use these tools in real situations can both help to develop the tools and help to develop understanding of the situations themselves. Care needs to be taken not to assume that all mathematics can be taught and learnt just by showing it in its practical guise: an example of this is methods of calculation. While it is clear that having methods of calculation at one's fingertips is useful for solving problems, it is also necessary to explore the calculation methods themselves in order to understand how they work. In doing so the study of the mathematics itself is the focus rather than its usefulness.

This chapter focuses on the practical application of mathematics to issues relevant to the global dimension and begins with a consideration of the benefits of this approach.

References

Cockcroft, WH. (1982) *Mathematics Counts: Report of the Committee of Inquiry into the Teaching of Mathematics in Schools.* London: HMSO.

DfES (1999) *The National Curriculum for Schools, Mathematics, Key Stages 1-4.* DfES: London

How the global dimension contributes to the teaching and learning of mathematics

Taking the present National Curriculum (DfES, 1999) as the default mathematics curriculum, it becomes clear that work based on the global dimension can contribute to all areas of mathematics.

Areas of *Ma1, Using and Applying Mathematics*, such as searching for patterns can be addressed by focusing on pattern making approaches applied in diverse cultures to the fabrics from which clothes and artefacts are made. In this context, the identification of different geometric shapes and how a range of rotation and reflection techniques have been applied can be studied and used. Additionally, learning how to play games devised by different cultures and developing strategies for winning helps to develop problem-solving skills as well as logical thinking.

Work in *Ma2, Number and the Number System* can derive from studying counting systems from diverse cultures and appreciating the use of place value, across many of these systems, as well as seeing how different cultures find different solutions to the same mathematical problems within their counting systems. Older pupils can benefit from learning about the development of the Hindu-Arabic counting system which is in common use in the west, as well as developing an awareness of different calculation methods which have been developed in other cultures, such as the *Gelosia* method of multiplication from India.

Much useful work in *Ma3, Shape Space and Measures* can arise from a global dimension, such as developing methods of mathematical translation of shapes to derive patterns such as Rangoli patterns, Islamic patterns and border patterns from the former Congo. Older pupils could benefit from studying some of the methods of geometry developed in Egypt and Ancient Greece.

Studying a range of issues deriving from the global dimension can give valuable opportunities to use data handling skills that come within *Ma4 Handling Data* such as analysis of charts and lists in making comparisons and being aware that data handling can be used mischievously by some to provide inaccurate or misleading interpretations.

How mathematics contributes to teaching and learning in the global dimension and to the development of children's global awareness

In considering the concepts underpinning the global dimension, mathematics appears to have a contribution to make to each although not necessarily equally. Mathematics can contribute significantly to global citizenship and diversity, by developing an understanding and an appreciation of:

- different ways of counting and structuring numbers
- games played in diverse cultures
- the significance of different geometric pattern making

This knowledge can encourage pupils to identify similarities and differences and make parallel connections across cultures. Older pupils could study some areas of the history of mathematics and identify the global connections and contributions that underpin mathematics in modern western cultures.

In considering the other key concepts of the global dimension, the contribution from mathematics tends to be different, largely coming from data handling tools. To ascertain the importance of issues being studied within these concepts, it is necessary to gather data, present data in a readable form (chart or graph), interpret data and come to conclusions based on data. It is hard to see how anyone can arrive at a full understanding of concepts such as interdependence or social justice or sustainable development, without well-developed data handling skills. An example of this type of investigation might be to gather data on present oil use, on likely remaining stocks and to use this to ascertain the estimated time remaining for oil-based economies.

Activities integrating mathematics into the global dimension.

The activities described in the following pages attempt to put this rationale into practice and focus on three distinct areas that contribute to the key ideas of global citizenship and diversity:

■ Area 1: Number

Context: The first activities focus on counting in languages other than English. The first part is aimed at Key Stage One or lower Key Stage Two and involves counting in Swahili, a language common to many African countries.

Activity 1: Counting in Swahili

Show children ten objects of some interest (e.g. shells, model cars, stuffed toys, conkers) and ask them to count them by chanting together.

Ask children if any of them can count in any language other than English.

Introduce the book *Moja Means One* (see Resources) and read it aloud, showing the illustrations and discussing with the children the similarities and differences between the environment of the book and their own surroundings.

Display the Swahili number names and encourage the children to chant them in order and in reverse order as they would 1-10 and 10-1 in English.

Get the children to count different sized sets of the objects from those counted at the beginning of the task.

Get the children to compile a booklet with a page focusing on each number. After some research to locate a range of objects linked to African countries (animals, artefacts) the children draw the number of artefacts matching the focus number for that page. They create their own Swahili counting book.

Extensions
■ Take a well-known number rhyme of song (eg Ten green bottles) and sing it with the Swahili numbers replacing the English ones. If other Swahili words can be found to replace English words then use these also – bottle is *chupa* in Swahili.

- See how many times you can bounce a ball and catch it but count in Swahili

- Play Show me your fingers but instead of using English 'Show me six fingers', use Swahili 'Show me *sita* (see-tah) Fingers'

- Ask for answers to simple addition and subtraction calculations but give the quantities in Swahili and expect the answers to be in Swahili too

- Use the companion book, *Jambo Means Hello: Swahili Alphabet Book* (see Resources) to explore the Swahili alphabet

- Undertake the same tasks but change the language

- If there are children in the class (or school) who speak another language, use that language; with the bonus that native speakers and so experts are on hand

- For older children it is useful to construct a hundred square using, for instance, Mandarin Chinese or Bengali characters and exploring how place value ideas are used in similar ways to those used in the Hindu-Arabic number system used in the west.

Resources

Feelings, M.(1979) *Moja Means One: Swahili Counting Book.* London: Puffin Books

Feelings, M.(1979) *Jambo Means Hello: Swahili Alphabet Book.* London: Puffin Books

Kampf, Marijn (2007) *Everything is 4* – www.marijn.org/everything-is-4/counting-0-to-100 Website containing information on counting from one to one hundred in twenty languages.

Several online dictionaries provide translation between English and other languages, including Swahili. On example is *Freedict* – www.freedict.com.

Wikipedia is a useful source for extending your subject knowledge in the area of counting in other number systems – http://en.wikipedia.org/wiki/Numeral_system

■ Area 2: Shape and space

These activities focus on spatial awareness in two dimensions. The initial focus explores pattern-making as used to construct border patterns in the former Congo, now Zaire.

Border Patterns

Context: Many cultures use simple or complex repeating patterns to decorate their surroundings and in some cases, these may have significant cultural or religious significance. Many of them make use of two-dimensional geometric shapes while others make use of the shapes supplied by nature in their surroundings. Repeating patterns at their simplest are those merely using translation, i.e. the same shape slid along to a different position without changing size, shape or orientation. Translation is the basis of many wallpapers and cloth designs. More complicated repeating patterns can be obtained by reflecting or rotating a basic shape to form a more complex shape which can then itself be subject to translation.

Activity

A first simple repeating pattern can be obtained by taking a simple geometric shape and repeating it in a line to form a border. This is the basis of many border patterns seen in Congolese artefacts (see Fugure 4). Children could use a ready-made shape or draw their own. An alternative would be to use a drawing program on computer to create the pattern and print it out – the drawing modules in *Microsoft Word* or *PowerPoint* would be appropriate or a an educational package, such as *Aspex Draw*.

A more complex pattern can be derived by taking a simple shape and rotating it 2 or 3 times to combine with the original shape. This combined shape can then be translated in the same way as before (see Figure 5). Again, a card shape drawn around is a good way to start but older and more ICT experienced pupils may wish to use a drawing package.

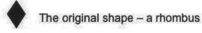
The original shape – a rhombus

A simple translation pattern for a border

A more complex translation pattern

Translation pattern using a non-geometric shape

Figure 4: Simple repeating patterns inspired by artefacts

The original shape – an arc of a circle

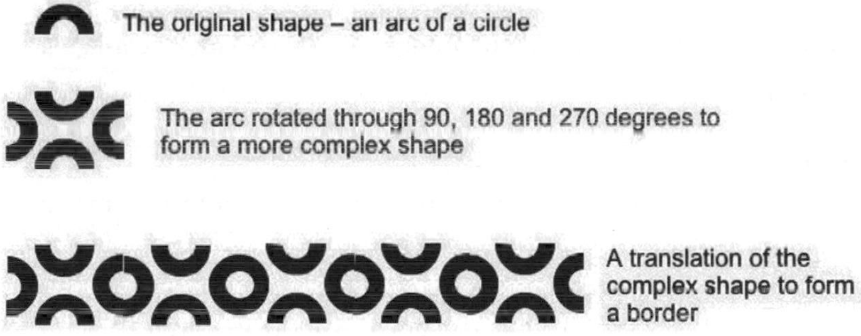

The arc rotated through 90, 180 and 270 degrees to form a more complex shape

A translation of the complex shape to form a border

Figure 5: More complex repeating patterns with rotation and translation.

Border patterns closer to the originals can be made by including more shapes and rotations to derive a more complex repeating unit – see below

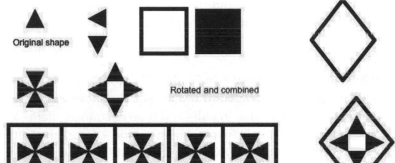
Original shape

Rotated and combined

Two border patterns formed by combining simple shapes and repeating them.

Figure 6: Examples using triangles, squares and rhombi

Resources

Card, paper, plastic geometric shapes to draw around

Drawing software eg the drawing modules in *Microsoft Word* or *PowerPoint* or *Aspex Draw*

Design Africa – www.design-africa.com/pattsBGs/patts02.html
Website displaying examples of Congolese and other African designs for materials, many using repeating pattern methods.

Zaslavsky, C. (1998) *Math games and activities from around the world*. Chicago: Chicago Review Press,

■ Area 3: Strategy games

Context: The focus in these activities is to encourage children to develop strategies for playing those games within the Three-in-a-Row family of which variations occur in many countries and which differ mainly in the design of the board on which the game is played.

Activities

Introduce the children to the game Noughts and Crosses, which is the simplest form of game of the Three-in-a-Row games. Allow some time for the children to play the game in pairs and then encourage them to identify which moves are helpful in playing the game. Discuss the fact that the game is played all over the world and provide them with some of the names given to the game in different countries – use the search term Tic-tac-toe in *Wikipedia* to find out these names.

Introduce the children to the family of Three-in-a-Row games that have versions throughout the world. A good start is Three Men's Morris (see below for board and rules) as it is simple and, once the principles are understood, can be applied to the range of games of this type.

Show the children two variations of the game such as *Shisima* from Kenya and Tapatan from the Philippines (see Resources).

Encourage children to devise strategies for winning the game by asking them to write down advice for someone who has not played the game before.

Have a *Shisima* or a *Tapatan* contest and ask the children to research the countries in which the games originated.

Extensions

The game of Nine Men's Morris is rewarding but it is more complex than any of the games discussed so far. However, children who have played and enjoyed the games in this section may well wish to try this more demanding game.

Research on the Web will reveal many other Three-in-a-Row games from other countries and each with their own particular board. Encourage children to locate these, draw the boards and play the games. How are they similar and how are they different from Nine Men's Morris?

Encourage the children to consider what other geometric shapes would make good boards for similar Three-in-a-row games. Suggest that they develop their own and play them.

For older children the game, *Mankala*, played throughout Africa has much potential. It is a distribution game rather than a three-in-a-row game with simple rules but can encourage the use of subtle strategies for winning.

Resources

The following websites provide background and more information on three in a row games:

Kellermeier, John. (2006) *Three-in-a-Row Games from around the World* – www.tacomacc.edu/home/jkellerm/MATH106/EthnomathematicsText/Chapter5/ThreeinaRowGames.htm
   Useful summary of Three-in-a-Row games and their various boards.

Kruzno (2005) *Row Games.* – www.kruzno.com/Rowgames.html

Details of *Shisima*, originating in Kenya, in which the pieces are called bugs because of their resemblance to water bugs moving over a body of water (*Shisima* means body of water). Also details of Tapatan, a game from the Philippines using a board similar to Three Men's Morris but with diagonals drawn in. The game is played in a similar way to *Shisima* except the 3-in-a-row can be any three adjacent vertices.

Three Men's Morris rules:

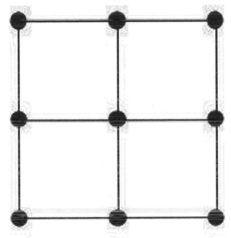

Figure 7: The Three Men's Morris board

Each of the two players has three counters of the same colour.

These are placed on the board one at a time with the players taking turns.

If one player succeeds in placing three of his/her counters in a row then this wins the game although this rarely happens as the other player blocks this.

Once all counters have been placed each player in turn moves one counter onto an adjacent empty point with the intention of achieving a three in a row.

When a player moves to form a three-in- a-row he or she may remove a counter belonging to the opponent and, since the opponent can no longer achieve a three-in-a-row, the game is won.

Shisima rules

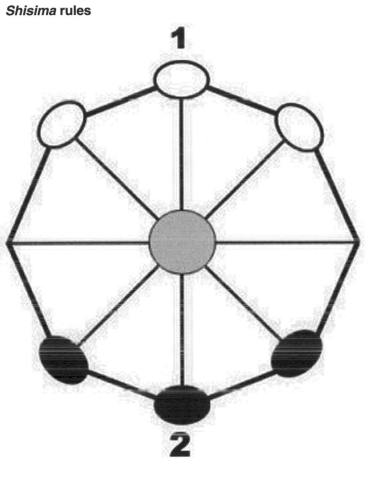

Figure 8: The Shisima board

Player one places the three bugs on the vertices marked 1 with player two doing the same on the vertices marked 2.

Each player in turn moves one bug to an adjacent empty vertex and this may include the one in the centre. A player has won once he or she has the three bugs in a straight line including the centre.

Chapter 5

Science and the global dimension

Jane Weavers

Rationale

Being part of the global community is an aspect of children's everyday life. The food they eat and clothes they wear are globally sourced; the media and festivals are increasingly international, giving many children some experience of aspects of diverse cultures and global issues.

Science research itself has a global perspective; ideas are shared and developed through the global scientific community. This has been the case for many years; the biological classification system, or medical advances such as the development of vaccines are examples of this. Despite the current western view of science; advance in scientific thinking has not always been the domain of the western world: most early scientific discoveries emanated from Asia.

Today, solutions once seen as only appropriate for less economically developed countries provide real alternatives for the whole world. For example, wind-up radios, which were initially developed to provide broadcast information in regions where power sources were not easily available, are now used in the developed world to provide an alternative source of energy.

Science seeks answers for many global issues. Current research focuses on such issues as:

- the development of food crops to alleviate starvation
- sources of sustainable energy to provide for the increasing world wide demand for energy and replacement of the diminishing supply of fossil fuels

■ methods of eradication of disease, including the development of drugs

■ early warning of the potentially catastrophic effect of extreme weather conditions

■ the need for both water for irrigation and clean drinking water for many developing countries

These are all areas that the scientific community is engaged in researching throughout the world. They are also issues which are comprehensible for primary-age children, who may have become familiar with them through the media and which will engage their concern and empathy. So we need to equip our children with the knowledge and understanding of how global issues can be informed and addressed by science. Children also need to understand the reality of the how their choices can impact on the rest of the world, and see that science can inform them about this, enabling them to make informed decisions. The ASE (2002) makes the case for teachers not to be afraid of addressing global issues in our science teaching:

> Science is a global activity with consequences for all our lives. It is also a human activity with ethical, social and political dimensions. Science education provides opportunities to relate technological change to changes in a wider context, such as effects on the environment and our quality of life. The impact of science is not confined to scientists but affects all people everywhere. (ASE, 2002)

In identifying the importance of Science, the National Curriculum for England in Key Stage One and Two (DfEE, 1999) recognises the global nature of science:

> Science stimulates and excited pupils' curiosity about phenomena and events in the world around them... Through science, pupils understand how major scientific ideas contribute to technological change – impacting on industry, business and medicine and improving the quality of life. Pupils recognise the cultural significance of science and trace its worldwide development. They learn to question and discuss science-based issues that may affect their own lives, the direction of society and the future of the world. (DFEE 1999)

Although this is the intention, in reality there is little indication of any requirement to explore the issues in a global context. The programmes of study outline little need to look outside the child's immediate experience of the world, and the impact of scientific phenomenon on themselves. Unfortunately, for primary-aged children the Science curriculum is often parochial, and whilst the subject knowledge and skills taught can be applied in a global context, often the reality of the experience is limited to context of school science and the children's immediate work rather than its application in the wider world. This can lead to a lack of understanding of the social relevance of Science in the world (Bourn, 2004). Science in the primary school needs to give children opportunities to look beyond their immediate horizons and realise their part in the global community.

Introducing a global aspect to Science in the primary school can provide many opportunities to apply scientific skills and knowledge in a real life context and broaden children's horizons. This encourages children to develop a wider view of global issues and provides potential motivation and engagement in science lessons.

References
Association for Science Education(ASE) (2002) *ASE Global – What is the global dimension?* Hatfield: ASE.

Bourn, D (2004) Development Education and Science Education. *School Science Review* 8

DfEE/QCA (1999) *The National Curriculum*. London, DfES

Further reading
Cutler, M (2007) *Sustainable Schools Through Science Across the World.* Primary Science Review 99

Peacock A, Symonds, L and Clegg, A (2006) Science Education across and beyond the United Kingdom. In Harlen, W. (ed) *ASE Guide to Primary Science Education.* Hatfield ASE.

The Association for Science Education Website has information about global science education – http://www.ase.org.uk/htm/ase_global/index1.php

Science across the World is a Website linking schools and teachers of science throughout the world – www.scienceacross.org

Background to the activities

The Science-based activities for Key Stage One and Two are around a theme of our impact on the global community. The Science National Curriculum has four distinct attainment targets, and whilst Sc1 permeates all science teaching, the other three focus on specific areas of science knowledge and understanding. For the purposes of this book a more thematic approach is adapted, with activities taken from across the attainment targets.

The first four activities are primarily aimed at Key Stage One children, although there are suggestions of development within them enabling them to be used with Key Stage Two children. The fifth activity on water is more appropriate for Key Stage Two; this is subdivided into a number of parts looking at different aspects.

■ Activity 1 – Similarities and Differences

To encourage children to recognise that we are part of the global community and whilst there are differences between us there are also many similarities in what we need. (Sc2 – life processes and living things)

Starting from the children's own experience, ask them to list what we need to live. It is likely that there will be a mix of things suggested which meet physiological and emotional needs and also things that are luxuries rather than needs.

This is an opportunity to discuss and explore these issues with children and to look at what children need in other environments, using resource materials from the suggested resource list. It should lead to the conclusion that for life to exist our physiological needs must be met. These are oxygen, food, water, and a relatively constant body temperature, which achieved through clothing and shelter. These are universal needs and although the ways in which they are met may differ throughout the global community, we all have the same basic needs. The need for nurture, care and friendship is also an important issue. Although this falls more into PSHE than science it opens up opportunities for cross-curricular links.

This activity could also be developed to look at the similarities and differences in animal life, taking opportunities to consider how the habitat affects what lives in a particular area.

■ Activity 2 – The clothes we wear

Clothing worn is strongly influenced by the region in which people live. While some of this influence is cultural and related to fashions, it is also strongly related to the type of materials available and climatic conditions.

Children will have worn different clothing at different times of the year and this often forms the basis for scientific investigation in school. It is easy to relate this to a more global perspective and look at the climatic conditions that children around the world live in and use this as a basis to investigate properties of materials and their suitability for clothing. This is related to the first activity, reinforcing the universal need for regulation of temperature and protection of the body, whilst also developing children's understanding of materials. (Sc3 Materials and their properties)

Using images (see Resources section), consider the clothing that is worn in different environments, identifying their properties and how they are related to the climatic conditions in the environment. This can lead into an investigation of the properties of materials used for clothing and how this is related to where people live.

Children can work in groups to plan and carry out investigations where they look at the clothing for a given environment such as the Arctic or a hot desert and consider the properties which are required. They will need to decide which property is most important and investigate it. Generally the insulating properties of the materials are explored for cooler environments. With older children, the colour of the clothing in hot environments and the effect this has on the absorption of heat can be investigated.

■ Activity 3 – Building materials

We need housing to provide shelter, but not all areas of the world have the same needs. Climate, available building materials and different construction techniques all play a part in determining the style of buildings used for homes. (Sc3 Materials and their properties)

The following activity considers the most appropriate building material for homes in different climates. Using pictures of different environments (see Resources section) such as hot desert, tropical rainforest or temperate forest, children can identify the climatic conditions and the materials available for building. This is similar to activity 3 in that it is looking at material properties, but is also a development in that two criteria need to be considered here, both what is suitable and what is available. This develops awareness of differences within the global community and raises economic considerations.

A development of this activity would be to look at the effects of extreme weather conditions in certain areas of the world and determine the factors to consider in the construction of buildings in different conditions.

■ Activity 4 – The food we eat

We need food to sustain us, but different cultures have different food preferences. This is partly dependent on being able to source food, looking at locally available foods and why some crops are grown in a particular environment. As with activity one, a common investigation carried out within Key Stage One involves planting seeds in a variety of conditions and finding out what is needed for successful growth. Developing this to look at global variations in food eaten and how this is related to environmental conditions is a valuable way of bringing a more global perspective to this investigation.

With Key Stage One children such investigations are most successful if carried out with a seed that grows comparatively quickly and easily such as mung beans and wheat are suitable for this. Beet crops and peanuts are other possibilities but take longer to grow. A potential development would be to consider some of the issues related to genetic modifications such as the development of 'Golden Rice'.

Key Stage Two focus

■ Activity 5 – Water for life

Based around the importance of water for life, there are a number of activities that children can carry out in the classroom looking at:

■ clean water

■ the effects of contaminated water

■ what is in water from different sources

■ ways of purifying water

■ ways in which water is sourced and transported to where it is needed

☐ Activity 5a – We all need water

Using reference materials and children's prior experiences establish why we need water for life. This is likely to lead to discussion of the need for water to enable us to grow food and the use of water for washing and cleaning which can affect health (Sc2 – life processes and living things).

These reasons for the need for water are the same throughout the global community, although looking at particular communities provides opportunities to consider what it means to have no clean water.

☐ Activity 5b – Clean water

Clean water is important for health and to limit spread of diseases, so it is important to look at methods of cleaning water. Many of these are possible to investigate in a primary school classroom, and different methods can be assessed for their effectiveness. (Sc3 Materials and their properties)

Children can develop their own ways of measuring whether their methods are successful. Possible methods of purification include:

■ filtration – various materials are used to filter water, using different types and sizes of filters such as fine sand and filter papers

■ chemical – Water purification tablets are easily available from camping shops and chemists

■ boiling

■ evaporation and condensation

■ solar disinfection – this is a method used in developing countries, in which small quantities of water are put into bottles and left in the full sun for about six hours. Research in 1991 (EAWAG and SANDEC http://www.sodis.ch/) showed it had potential to improve health where clean water was not freely available. It works through heating and ultra violet radiation

☐ Activity 5c – What is in water?

The water from our taps is purified, but there is an increasing demand for bottled water. Marketing it focuses on the fact that it is purer and thus better for us. Any measure of water quality depends on what the water is going to be used for. Pure water is water with no contaminant in it, so any measure is likely to involve looking at a range of factors.

In the primary classroom factors such as how clear the water is can be looked at qualitatively by making visual judgements. For greater accuracy, a quantitative measure using a light meter or data logger to measure the amount of light passing through a fixed amount of water can be used. It is also possible to measure the pH or alkalinity of water using indicators. (Sc3 Materials and their properties)

Consideration of what is in water can raise the issues of fluoride being added to water.

☐ Activity 5d – Pumping water

Work on forces invites the exploration of hydraulic pumps, giving children the opportunity to look at ways of pumping water.

This could be developed to include looking of ways of powering pumps, which for the developing world may include methods such as solar powered pumps, which can be explored in the classroom using simple solar cells. (Sc4 Physical processes)

Resources for the activities

Books

Holly, B (1999) *Wake Up, World! A day in the life of children around the world.* London: Frances Lincoln

Kroll, V (1994) *Masai and I.* London: Puffin Books

UNICEF (2006) *A Life Like Mine.* London: Dorling Kindersley Publishers Ltd

Also the *Around the World* series and *Child's Day* series from Frances Lincoln Children's Books

Other resources you will need

Good quality images of clothing and buildings in a range of environments are available from several Web sites, suitable for primary school use. Examples include:

Images of the World – www.imagesoftheworld.org

Staffordshire Learning Net Geography Images – www.sln.org.uk/geography/Images.htm

Geography Photos – www.geographyphotos.com

The Geography Site Image Gallery – www.geography-site.co.uk

You can also locate suitable images by searching and downloading images from a photo-sharing service, such as *Flickr* – www.flickr.com

A variety of clothing and building materials are usually available within schools but if necessary packs of materials can be obtained from school suppliers: seeds can also be ordered.

Chapter 6

Geography and the global dimension

Wendy Garner

In the morning we drink coffee provided for us by a South American, or tea by a Chinese, or cocoa by a West African. Before we leave for our jobs we're already indebted to more than half the world.
– Martin Luther King

Rationale

Events across the world are more interrelated than they first appear. We all live on one planet and almost every part of our lives is linked in some way or another to the land, sea, and air that form our world; a world we share with everyone else – some six billion other people! In essence, geography as a subject encompasses all aspects of our planet and the ways in which people interact with its land, sea and air.

Developing the global dimension through geography is about exploring the world at a human level. For example, when studying a distant locality, concepts such as interdependence can be introduced. Rather than just learning about the distant locality itself, children can explore connections between the distant place and the one they call home. Issues surrounding resources can be investigated in both places. Exploring the issue of fair trade can help children to recognise that some links between localities can be exploitative, thus giving meaning and context to the concept of social justice. The activities for Key Stage One focus on fair trade issues in the context of a distant locality.

However there are problems associated with, what is sometimes called a camera zoom-lens approach to distant locality studies. Although comparisons with localities of a similar size to the school locality are relevant and meaningful, children need to develop an awareness of the wider geographical context alongside in-depth insights into the lives of people within a specific location. The activities below for Key Stage Two focus on significant world events within the context of developing a locational framework.

Encouraging children to take a critical stance will enhance their geographical understandings and skills. Enquiry is a key skill in learning and teaching geography and is how children become young geographers, enabling them to engage in problem-solving and reach reasoned conclusions. Such constructivist, participatory methods are essential to the development of children's global perspectives.

In terms of the content of the National Curriculum, there are various opportunities to develop global concepts, themes and issues. Apart from conventional locality studies and the study of people in those places, thematic aspects such as environmental management and sustainable development are key elements within the requirements.

Activities

Key Stage One Contrasting Locality Study: Fair trade as a global issue

Rationale

This sequence of activities relates to the requirement at Key Stage One to study a contrasting locality. The ideas suggested could be incorporated within a more comprehensive unit of work on a specific locality within an economically developing country. The theme of Fair Trade has been chosen as it is directly relevant to children's daily lives as members of the global community. The production and sale of everyday commodities such as clothes, food and drink are central to the issue. Increasingly, most high street stores and supermarkets have some stock of Fair Trade produce. There are now over 2000 Fair Trade certified products in the UK and a good range of resources is available to support the teaching of Fair Trade issues (see Resources section).

Children's engagement with a global issue such as this presents an excellent context for purposeful and meaningful geographical enquiry. Also, children can start to consider underpinning concepts such as interdependence and higher order concepts such as social justice. It has been argued earlier that some concepts relating to the global dimension need to be explored before others, that some concepts represent a lens through which others can be viewed. Within this series of activities it is proposed that children be encouraged to explore the idea of interdependence before touching on ideas relating to social justice and human rights. Clearly, other concepts will be touched upon and developed to some extent but it is useful to identify the strong links in terms of focused planning.

■ Activity 1 – Let's go shopping!

As a stimulus, a display could be generated by the teacher and children showing food packaging and origin. Not all packaging shows where food is produced, but vegetables and fruit packaging often include this information or your local greengrocer could be consulted. There may be other items, such as clothing, which could be added to the display. Links could be made to a large world map or globe.

This would be an excellent point at which to share the story *The World Came to My Place Today* by Jo Readman and Ley Honor Roberts, a picture book published by Eden Project Books (2002) (see Chapter 2), with a view to introducing the concept of interdependence and how we are linked to other people and places across the world.

■ Activity 2 – Is it fair?

Within this activity, the concept of interdependence will be developed and social justice will be touched upon in terms of the welfare of all people, particularly producers.

As a stimulus, introduce a bag of shopping containing a range of Fair Trade products. Alternatively download and print photographs of the full range of retail products from the Fairtrade Web site (see Resources section). The range of products is wide and includes items relevant to children such as chocolate, sweets, cereal, clothes and cakes.

Highlight the areas of Africa, Asia, Latin America and the Caribbean on a world map and explain to the children that these places supply the UK market with Fair Trade certified products. To encourage children to think about mapping and concepts such as distance, ask about how the products might be transported and the length of time it would take. Show the children a bar of Fair Trade chocolate and allow them to have a taste. Explain that the main ingredient of chocolate is cocoa, which is the seed from a tree that is farmed mainly in West Africa.

Now show a bar of chocolate that is not certified as Fair Trade. Engage the children in discussion about how the chocolate bar reaches us and who earns the most and least, given the price the consumer pays. This should emphasise the differences in monies gained by cocoa farmers, the chocolate maker, tax collectors and retailers. Ask the children to discuss whether they think this is fair.

> For a typical 50p bar of chocolate that is not Fair Trade certified, the split in monies is as follows: 3p to the cocoa farmer, 3p for transport (from farm to port and by ship to the UK), 20p to the chocolate maker in the UK, 14p to the retailer and 10p in tax.
>
> For Fair Trade chocolate, the split is the same, but as the chocolate maker in the UK is part owned by cocoa farmers, about one third (7p) of the 20p earned by the chocolate maker goes to the farmer.
>
> Source: Divine Chocolate Ltd.

■ Activity 3 – What is being done?

Prior to a hot seating activity where the teacher will be in role as a Fair Trade producer (see Resources), ask the children to research and prepare questions using photographs, objects and prior knowledge. Arrange them in a horseshoe with the teacher in the centre. Children are invited to ask questions to which the teacher – in role – responds in a way that encourages further questioning. The class could produce a simple mind map of all they have learnt about Fair Trade.

■ Activity 4 – What can we do?

In conclusion, children could produce posters to display around the school, encouraging the purchase of Fair Trade products. A Fair Trade stall could be established and a tasting session could be arranged when pupils give short, simple presentations about why they think Fair Trade products should be purchased.

Resources for the activities

Websites

Fair Trade Foundation – www.fairtrade.org.uk
   Good source of information about Fair Trade, producers, products and how to become a Fair Trade School.

Reading International Solidarity Centre – www.risc.org.uk
   A range of resources relating to trade in general and Fair Trade.

Traidcraft – www.traidcraft.co.uk
   A trading company and a development charity centrally concerned with the distribution of Fair Trade food, crafts and clothing.

Key Stage Two – Our World: Past, Present and Future

This sequence of activities relates to the QCA geography scheme of work units Passport to the World and In the News. The two units aim to develop children's awareness of the wider world. Within this section, specific concepts relating to the global dimension will be fused within activities, which help to develop children's world knowledge and international understanding. The concepts addressed overlap, underpin and interrelate with each other, but the strongest links have been highlighted for the purposes of focused planning.

It is envisaged that this is a continuous or on-going unit. The suggested activities do not need to be taught consecutively or necessarily in the suggested order. They can effectively stand alone or be integrated within other curriculum areas or cross-curricular projects.

Three perspectives have been taken which relate to the past, the present and the future. This is because much of what is discussed in terms of the global dimension is concerned with reflection on past events, consideration of current issues and implications for our future.

■ Activity 1 – Peacemakers from the past

This activity aims to introduce ideas relating to conflict resolution. The curriculum contexts include geography, history and Religious Education.

Introduce the activity by asking the children to find out which nations were involved in World War One and to find some of these places on a world map. Ask children to use an atlas and the Web to find out about Belgium and the location of Flanders.

Tell the children the story of what happened on the stroke of midnight, Christmas Eve 1914 (see Resources). Describe how an informal truce was struck between young British and German soldiers, which took the form of singing carols, exchanging gifts and even playing football. Explain how the truce was shortlived as the generals moved many of the soldiers involved, but that this is an example of peacemaking and the promotion of harmony on a small scale.

Organise children into small groups and brief each group to research and present findings on other peace makers through time and across the world. These may include figures such as Martin Luther King, Gandhi or Nelson Mandela. Locate people and events on a displayed timeline and world map.

■ Activity 2 – Issues for today

This activity aims to introduce ideas relating to global citizenship, interdependence and sustainable development. The curriculum contexts include geography and science.

Introduce the concept of sustainability, building on children's prior learning. Ask children to design a logo for sustainability at a global level. This could be in the form of a school competition with the winner having their design published in a school newsletter.

Discuss the issue of oil and food prices with the children (see Resources for Briefing Sheet). Identify key issues, such as:

■ Why is oil an important source of fuel?

■ Who are the main oil consumers? Where are the main oil reserves?

■ What is the link between fossil fuels, such as oil and global warming and climate change?

■ How have governments sought to reduce their countries' oil consumption?

Children could complete concept maps in relation to some of these ideas.

Arrange a class debate with different groups in role. For example, oil producer, manufacturing company, car owner, environmental activist, and so on. Ask children to prepare to present their view, in role, of whether the solution of biofuel is a good one. From a personal perspective discuss how the children can respond to these issues as responsible citizens.

BRIEFING SHEET – OIL AND FOOD PRICES

Oil has long been a very important source of fuel for everything from heating, producing electricity and petrol for vehicles. It is also the main ingredient for producing modern materials such as plastics, synthetic fibres, paints and many other products we take for granted. Oil is found under the ground and sea, but only in certain parts of the world. It is a finite resource and once oil supplies cannot keep up with demand then the price of oil will rise considerably.

Traditionally the rich, industrialised nations of North America, Europe and Japan have been the main oil consumers but only North America, the United Kingdom and Norway have oil reserves within their territories. Much of the world's oil reserves are to be found in the Middle East and Russia (a growing oil producer).

In the past few decades manufacturing businesses have changed radically from supplying their local domestic markets with goods to competing with one another to supply goods anywhere in the world. Cheap oil for low cost transportation of goods and modern digital technologies have enabled this to happen. Many businesses have bought up competitors and have grown to dominate the world's markets. Those who can manufacture for the least cost win so there has been a more recent trend, particularly from the 1990s onwards, to move manufacture to countries where people are poor and will work for much less money, China being the most outstanding example. In the past 15 years China has developed from being a closed communist state to being the world's second largest producer of manufactured goods. As a result, the Chinese population (one fifth of the world's) is becoming wealthier and acquiring the same goods as the industrialised countries – cars, televisions, fridges, air conditioning, etc. This is leading to China consuming much more oil.

Over the past two decades there has been a growing worry about global warming and climate change caused by all the carbon dioxide gases entering the atmosphere directly from burning fossil fuels such as coal, gas and oil. The world's weather patterns appear to be changing. Amongst the many effects of this are catastrophic weather events harming people and their crops. Governments around the world are now trying to limit climate change by seeking agreements across all major industrialised countries to reduce their consumption of carbon-based fossil fuels. Unfortunately, the industrialisation of countries like China is leading to these countries increasing their oil consumption at a much faster rate than it is thought possible for established industrialised nations to reduce their consumption. Alternative sources of energy are needed.

Thus globalisation of business has led western businesses to move production to the east, which has made these countries more industrialised and taken away from the west the control of oil consumption and the theoretical ability to tackle climate.

One of the ways in which western governments have sought to reduce their countries' oil consumption has been to develop fuel oils produced from plants, known as biofuel, to replace some of the oil used in petrol and diesel for vehicles. Governments have provided subsidies for biofuel to encourage this. As the plants grown to produce the oil take carbon dioxide out of the atmosphere, burning this oil should only be putting the same gas back into the atmosphere again rather than adding to it, as would be the case with fossil fuels. The idea seemed a good one. However, as farmers have shifted from growing cereal crops for food production to growing crops for biofuel less food is being produced. Prices of basic cereals have risen considerably around the world (cereals and other basic foods are now traded globally just like manufactured goods) and food shortages have arisen in the poorer parts of the world. Fuel and food now compete for arable land. This increases the incentive to clear more land for agriculture, which means increasing deforestation.

Food shortages and conflicts in the interests of different countries could lead to more political instability in poorer countries and greater risks of civil unrest and war.

Thus an attempt on a world scale to tackle global warming via biofuels has led to more forest burning, food shortages, and more political instability across the world: this is opposite of what was envisaged. The world is a limited space with limited resources, which we all share. Oil and food prices are now closely linked.

■ Activity 3 – What about tomorrow?

As a homework activity, ask children to collect images of the future conveyed in books, comics, newspapers and computer games. In the classroom, in small groups, ask children to share their findings and list images they have found of the future. Display findings.

Show children two books by Jeannie Baker: *Where the Forest Meets the Sea* and *Window* (see Resources). These portray key aspects of change over time in different environments. Discuss the changes they have noted.

Undertake an art activity where children are asked to split their page in half and on one side draw what they think the probable future will be like for the planet and on the other, their preferred future. Ask some groups to focus on their personal future, some on the local area and others to take a global perspective. When complete, discuss how this relates to the images of the future portrayed by the sources they bought into school. Ask the children to list differences between their probable and preferred futures and to identify ways in which their ideal future can be achieved.

Resources

Books

Baker, Jeannie. (1989) *Where the Forest Meets the Sea.* London: Walker Books

Baker, Jeannie. (2002) *Window.* London: Walker Books

McCutcheon, John and Sorensen, Henri. (2006) *Christmas in the Trenches (with Audio CD).* Atlanta, Georgia: Peachtree Publishers

Pax Christi (1999) *Year in Year out: Twelve Stories about Peacemakers.* London: Pax Christi

Chapter 7

History and the global dimension

Tony Pickford

History, as defined by the English National Curriculum in Key Stages One and Two and the corresponding area of learning and development in the Early Years Foundation Stage curriculum, offers great opportunities for developing children's skills and understanding in relation to the concepts of the global dimension. As a subject it is fundamentally concerned with evidence and its interpretation – Cooper (2000) describes what a historian does in the following terms:

> Historians investigate the past by interpreting traces of the past, the evidence. They interpret evidence through a process of deductive reasoning, but evidence is often incomplete, and for this and other reasons, more than one interpretation may be defensible.

The skills and processes implicit in this description appear in the programme of study for history as Skills, knowledge and understandings, labelled as Key Elements in earlier versions of the documentation. This provides the framework for children's study of history and characterise it as a subject which is fundamentally concerned with open-minded, informed investigation and enquiry. As well as developing chronological understandings, history is informed by core concepts: change and continuity, cause and effect, similarity and difference, processes of interpretation and evidential skills, through the analysis of sources.

Historical concepts, processes and skills are clearly applicable to the principles of collaborative, active learning that underpin the concepts of the global dimension: they also offer a distinctive lens through which to view global issues. Questions used for analysis of historical sources such as What does the source tell me, How certain can I be, What can I infer? What are the reasons for the viewpoint it offers? provide a rigorous and distinctive set of tools for unpicking sources related to global issues. They are vital to conceptual development about values and perceptions, particularly in detecting bias in sources from the media.

However, the subject knowledge content of the National Curriculum for history in England raises some issues in relation to the global dimension. Apart from two areas of study at Key Stage Two, the required history curriculum and the corresponding area of learning in the Early Years Foundation Stage curriculum are focused on British history, with an emphasis on personal, family and local history for the youngest children. The Foundation Stage requirements, in particular, are parochial in their scope, dealing only with children's experiences and the perspectives of adults whom they know. Although the increasing diversity of communities means that global perspectives can be accessed through family and local links, the statutory curriculum lends itself to an insular view of history. Woodhouse (2002) argues that the Foundation stage curriculum should be extended into 'the unfamiliar context of a long time ago'. She states:

> Do not be afraid of introducing children to much earlier historical periods: the 'big' contrasts between daily life now and a hundred or more years ago can actually be easier for young children to understand. Topics such as castles can capture children's imagination and interest precisely because life was so very different from their own experiences today. (Woodhouse, 2002)

Similarly, the insular focus of Key Stage Two units, such as Victorian Britain, can be opened up to wider perspectives by the inclusion of significant individuals and events with global links, such as Mary Seacole and her work during the Crimean War. The example for Key Stage Two takes one of the World Study units required by the programme of study, the Aztecs, and shows how well-chosen sources can be used to develop critical thinking and interpretation skills.

References

Cooper H (2000) The Teaching of History in Primary Schools – Implementing the Revised National Curriculum. London: David Fulton

Woodhouse A (2002) Learning about the past in the foundation stage. Primary History Matters, Spring, 31, p2-8 Winchester: Hampshire County Council

Key Stage 1
A Famous Person: Rosa Parks

Rationale

Rosa Parks is among the list of famous people suggested in the introduction to the QCA history scheme of work unit 4 'Why do we remember Florence Nightingale?' Although she is not the only person in the list from beyond the UK or from an ethnic minority background (Mary Seacole and Pocahontas both feature), she is particularly significant in that her fame arose from her brave and direct response to discrimination and injustice. Her story is related to key themes and concepts of the global dimension, including social justice, human rights and conflict resolution.

Although relatively unknown in the UK, Rosa is famous in the United States as a black campaigner and civil rights activist. She was a contemporary and friend of Dr Martin Luther King. The act for which she is best remembered is her refusal to give up her seat in the 'Whites Only' section of a segregated bus in Montgomery, Alabama in December, 1955. This action led to her arrest, a boycott of buses by the black community in Montgomery and eventually, to racial segregation on buses being declared unconstitutional by the US Supreme Court a year later. The story is told by several sources – see Resources below. Although suggested as an appropriate topic for Key Stage One, Rosa's story involves ideas and concepts, such as discrimination and segregation, which require some explanation and exploration by children.

In the fifties, under what were known as 'Jim Crow Laws', the segregation of black people and white characterised virtually every aspect of daily life in the southern states of the USA. Blacks were disadvantaged in every respect – for example, on public transport such as buses, although they accounted for more than 75 per cent of passengers, they were restricted to sections at the rear of vehicles. These sections were not fixed in size but were determined by the placement of a movable sign. Black people could sit in the middle rows, but when the white section at the front was full, they had to move to seats at the rear, stand, or, if there was no room, leave the bus. In Rosa's case, she was in a seat in the middle section of a bus, which became designated Whites Only, when the sign was moved to accommodate an influx of white passengers. Her choice was to move to the back, like other black passengers in her section, or stay in her seat and risk arrest for breaking city laws. Her decision to stay in the seat is often attributed to tiredness at the end of a busy day, but Rosa described the reason for her action, as follows:

> People always say that I didn't give up my seat because I was tired, but that isn't true. I was not tired physically, or no more tired than I usually was at the end of a working day. ... No, the only tired I was, was tired of giving in.

The extent of segregation at the time is best illustrated by images – see Resources – which clearly indicate its pervasiveness in society. A practical activity may be useful to help children understand the nature of discrimination and segregation and the feelings they engender. After a briefing to explain the nature of the activity, split the class into two groups for some entirely arbitrary reason, not on gender or physical characteristics. You can use an equally split set of cards, from which the children choose, marked with two symbols – perhaps, noughts and crosses. Once the children are split into two groups, over the period of a few lessons, give privileges to one group and not the other: the noughts group could be allowed out at playtime before the others for example. At the end of the activity, carefully debrief the children to bring out the emotions and feelings engendered for both groups by the activity. Focus on the feelings of the disadvantaged group, particularly the frustration they felt at being denied basic choices and equal treatment.

Another aspect of the story that will need some explanation is the black people's boycott of buses that followed Rosa's arrest. The term may be unfamiliar to children but the concept of a boycott is simple to explain. The key point to make is that the boycott was not an easy option. As most black people in Montgomery had no other form of transport to get to work or do other essential tasks, the boycott led to hardship for the black community as well as for the bus company. Rosa's story also raises a significant issue about the law and the need to defy laws which are unjust. This is a complicated moral issue, well beyond the remit of this book, but Dr Martin Luther King's views on the subject are worthy of note. Below is an extract from his *Letter from Birmingham Jail* from April 1963:

> How does one determine whether a law is just or unjust? A just law is a man-made code that squares with the moral law or the law of God. An unjust law is a code that is out of harmony with the moral law. To put it in the terms of St. Thomas Aquinas: An unjust law is a human law that is not rooted in eternal law and natural law. Any law that uplifts human personality is just. Any law that degrades human personality is unjust. All segregation statutes are unjust because segregation distorts the soul and damages the personality. It gives the segregator a false sense of superiority and the segregated a false sense of inferiority.

The outline on pages 53-58 features a hot seating activity in which children pose questions for someone taking on the role of Rosa. This could be an adult or a group of children. In both cases, Rosa's answers can be firmly based on her genuine feelings and views. Some of the Web sites, listed in the Resources section, feature detailed interviews with her in which she responds to most of the questions children are likely to raise. A group of children, taking on the role of Rosa Parks, could use the interviews to research their responses to questions before the hot seating activity.

Resources

As well as her autobiography (published in 1999), which has been adapted for younger readers, there are several books, which tell Rosa Parks's story for a younger audience. Sources include:

- Parks, R and Haskins, J (1999) *Rosa Parks: My Story.* Puffin

- Edwards, P and Shanahan, D (2005) *The Bus Ride That Changed History: The Story of Rosa Parks.* Houghton Mifflin

- Ringgold, F (2003) *If a Bus Could Talk: The Story of Rosa Parks.* Aladdin Paperbacks

- Steele, P (2007) *Rosa Parks and Her Protest for Civil Rights.* (Dates with History series) Cherrytree Books

- Wilson, C (2001) *Rosa Parks* (Scholastic Biography series). Leamington Spa: Scholastic

The story of Rosa's protest and her later life is also told on several Web sites, some featuring interviews with her in audio and/or video.

- Rosa and her husband founded the *Rosa and Raymond Parks Institute for Self Development* in 1987. Its Website features an outline biography, which places the events of 1955-6 into context. www.rosaparks.org

- Rosa's entry in *Wikipedia* is protected from alteration by users and can be considered as an authoritative account of her life, focusing in some detail on the events on the bus in Montgomery and their aftermath. http://en.wikipedia.org/wiki/Rosa_Parks

- The entry in the US Academy of Achievement Web site features an interview and a photo gallery. On the Home page, find *Parks, Rosa* in the 'Select Achiever' drop-down list. www.achievement.org

- Although aimed at an older audience than Key Stage One, the US Scholastic Web site features a detailed account of her achievements and an interview aimed at a younger audience. http://teacher.scholastic.com/rosa

For images relating to segregation in the southern USA in the fifties, go to *Photographs of Racial Segregation Signs* on the About.com Web site. http://afroamhistory.about.com/od/jimcrowlaw1/ig/Racial-Segregation-Signs/index.htm

Outline planning for a sequence of lessons for Year 2 – The Story of Rosa Parks

Objectives *By the end of the activity pupils will be able to ...*	Content	Resources	Assessment for Learning *Can a pupil ... ?*
1. Identify some people from the past and present who are famous 2. Empathise with a historical character at a simple level.	■ What does famous mean? Get the children to name some famous people that they know and identify why they are famous. ■ Show a picture of Rosa Parks in 1955 and explain that she is a woman who is famous for doing a very brave act. This happened many years ago in another country – the United States of America – at a time when black people, like Rosa, were treated differently from white people. Introduce and explain the term, segregation. ■ Locate Rosa on a timeline (born February 1913, became famous in December 1955, died October 2005). ■ Tell the first part of the story up to the arrest and the decision to boycott the buses in Montgomery. ■ Discuss with the children Rosa's feelings at points in the story when she got on the bus after a day at work; when the sign was moved to indicate that her section of the bus was now Whites Only: when the bus driver told her to move; after her arrest. ■ **Activity**: Children write sentence/s about how they would feel in Rosa's place at a point in the story that they choose. ■ **Plenary**: Share some of the children's sentences.	Timeline Picture of Rosa Parks in 1955	■ Identify a famous person and a reason for their fame ■ Identify Rosa's feelings at a point in the story.

Outline planning for a sequence of lessons for Year 2 – The Story of Rosa Parks (continued)

Objectives	Content	Resources	Assessment for Learning
By the end of the activity pupils will be able to ...			*Can a pupil ... ?*
	■ Recap story so far.		
	■ Remind children about life for black people in the southern United States in 1955. Look at the pictures showing evidence of segregation.	Images from *Photographs of Racial Segregation Signs* on the About.com Web site.	
3. Sequence pictures and sentences from a story about a real person	■ Tell the second part of story up to the Supreme Court decision and Rosa riding at the front of a Montgomery bus for the first time.		
4. Empathise with a historical character at a simple level.	■ Show the image of Rosa's first bus ride at the front of a bus. Ask the children to describe the picture and what Rosa's feelings might have been on that day and why she is not smiling in the picture.	Image of Rosa at the front of a bus – *Academy of Achievement* Web site is one of many possible sources.	■ Order events in the story correctly ■ Identify Rosa's feelings at a point in the story.
	■ **Activity**: In groups, sequence pictures and then sentences from the story (extension task – get the children to add their own sentences to describe the pictures).	Pictures and sentence 'cards' – Photocopiables 1 and 2.	
	■ **Plenary**: Children share their own sentences.		

Outline planning for a sequence of lessons for Year 2 – The Story of Rosa Parks (continued)

Objectives *By the end of the activity pupils will be able to ...*	Content	Resources	Assessment for Learning *Can a pupil ... ?*
5. Identify different perspectives in a story about a famous person. 6. Raise questions for an historical figure.	■ Recap story – question children about the main points. ■ List some of the people in the story on board – Rosa, the bus driver, Dr King, etc. ■ Ask the children to think about what Rosa and others might have said at different points in the story. ■ **Activity**: Group writing – in small groups, children take key events in the story and agree on statements to put in speech bubbles. ■ **Plenary**: What questions would you have liked to ask Rosa about her life? List questions.	Picture 'cards' – Photocopiable 1	■ Identify the views of a participant in Rosa Parks's story. ■ Raise a question about Rosa's life.
7. Ask questions for an historical figure. 8. Identify a reason why Rosa Parks is famous.	■ 'Hot seating' activity – an adult or a group children (taking on the role of Rosa Parks) answer questions raised in the previous activity. ■ Answers are recorded by simple note-taking. ■ **Plenary**: Get the children to identify reasons why Rosa Parks is famous. Record children's reasons. **Extension**: Not many people in the UK know about Rosa Parks. Get the children to identify ways in which they could make people more aware of Rosa and her story. Children could make posters, a class book, a short video or an assembly for the rest of the school.	(Research by adult or children taking audio or video recording. on the role of Rosa Parks using interviews on Web sites)	■ Identify a reason why Rosa Parks is famous.

Photocopiable 1 – Pictures from the Story of Rosa Parks

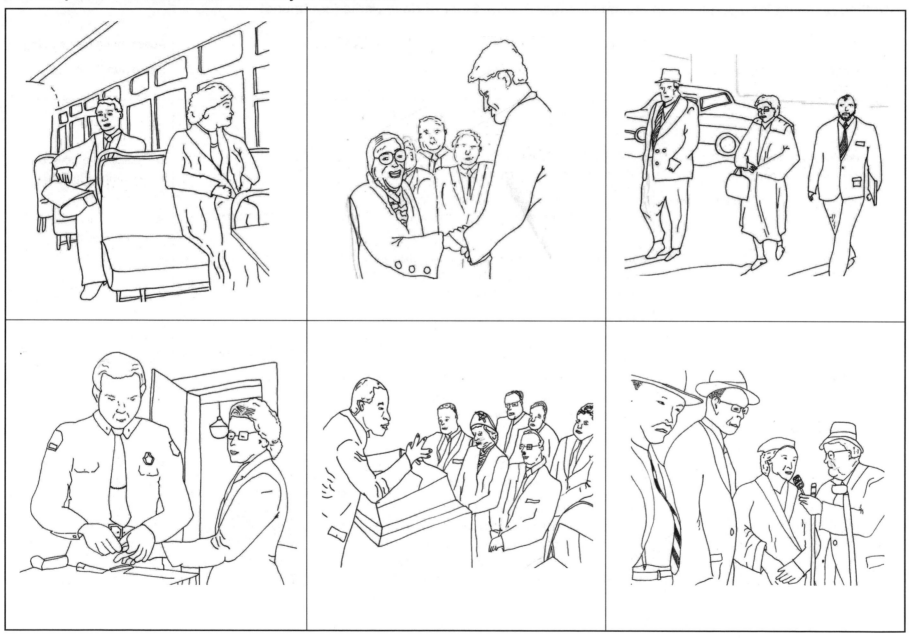

Photocopiable 2 – The Story of Rosa Parks

Rosa became famous and news reporters wanted to talk to her.	Rosa went to a meeting where Doctor King talked about making life better for black people.	After her arrest, Rosa's fingerprints were taken by the police.
After her arrest, Rosa went to court and was found guilty of breaking the law.	When she was older, Rosa met the President of the United States. He thanked her for her brave act in 1955.	After the law was changed, Rosa sat at the front of a bus for the first time.

Photocopiable 3 – The Story of Rosa Parks – *Simpler Captions*

News reporters asked Rosa questions.	Rosa went to hear Doctor King speak.	Rosa's fingerprints were taken.
Rosa went to court.	When she was older, Rosa met the President.	Rosa sat at the front of a bus for the first time.

Key Stage 2
World Study: The Aztecs

■ Activity 1 – A Time Capsule
Rationale

An appropriate starting point for a Study Unit such as The Aztecs, which is based upon archaeological evidence, is an investigation into the nature of the evidence itself. This clearly makes the point that only a restricted picture of everyday life is provided by a limited array of evidence.

Activity

It is the year 2500, 500 years from now and the children are a group of archaeologists who have discovered a bag of artefacts from the early 21st century. The bag is presented to the children and key points are made about its value and the importance of treating it and its contents with care. Give the children *Photocopiable 4* and tell them to record any information about early 21st Century life that they can deduce from the contents of the bag. Remind them that, as future archaeologists, they know little about the period but can read written English from the time. Get the children to explore the contents of the time capsule in groups or you could set up the examination of the contents as a teacher-led, whole class activity. The bag should contain a range of pieces of evidence, but essential items include:

- an itemised supermarket till receipt or shopping list of everyday food items
- packet foods, such as soup or sauces
- an unlabelled can of food, e.g. beans or soup
- a pair of earrings or other item of jewellery
- an art gallery guide
- a music CD and a video/DVD of a film or TV programme
- a newspaper
- a TV listings magazine
- a calendar, with religious festivals
- a coin

Taken together, these items provide clues about early 21st century life and some notes can be made under all of the headings on *Photocopiable 4*. However, evidence is limited and the items raise as many questions as they answer – for example, the till receipt gives good details of the range of foods purchased, but does not tell us if everyone ate in this way or whether this was a stock of food for a day, a week or a month. At the end of the activity, debrief the children about what they have discovered and draw out key points about inadequate evidence and the need to fill in gaps by deduction and interpretation. Make the point that the Aztec civilisation is as distant in time from now as we are from future archaeologists. Ask the children when – if ever –they think the evidence about the Aztecs will be complete.

■ Activity 2 – Finding out about the Aztecs

Rationale

In this activity, children use the same structured recording sheet to gather evidence about the Aztecs as they used to record and interpret the contents of the time capsule box or bag. This links the two activities and continues the theme of interpreting limited and incomplete evidence.

Activity

Introduce the Aztec civilisation in time and space – locate on a timeline: the civilisation was at its height when encountered by the Spanish in 1519, but had been in existence for over 300 years. Use a world map or globe to locate the capital city of the Aztec Empire which was called Tenochtitlan (Cactus Rock in English) and was located on the site of present-day Mexico City. Although described as an Empire, the Aztec lands did not compare in extent to, for example, the Roman Empire or the British Empire because although the Aztecs conquered many local tribes in the central plain of Mexico, they did not venture further. Introduce *Photocopiable 4* again and set the task of finding out about everyday Aztec life, using the headings as a structure. Depending on the children's research skills, either get them to gather information under all of the headings or assign particular headings to groups of collaborative researchers. A range of resources are available for independent research by children in Key Stage Two (see Resources section): the *Snaith Primary School* Website – http://home.freeuk.net/elloughton13/aztecs.htm – is particularly clear, informative and extensive.

Careful debriefing of the children will be essential at the end of the allotted time for research. Many sources about the Aztecs stress the strangeness (to us) of their lifestyle, especially in relation to religious beliefs: they had a uniquely pessimistic religion, which emphasised the importance of the shedding of blood and sacrifice to continue the cycle of night and day. Other aspects of life, though strange to us, are comparable to attitudes in Europe in the sixteenth century – for example, the strict rules relating to the clothes that could be worn by people at different levels of society, with harsh punishments for transgression are similar to rules prevalent in Elizabethan England. Draw the children's attention to other aspects of everyday life, which indicate a sophisticated, highly developed society – for example, the size and extent of Tenochtitlan, the striking works of Aztec art and the system of *chinampas* (individual smallholdings) which meant that people at all levels of society had a healthier and more varied diet than their counterparts in Europe at the time.

■ Activity 3 – The Spanish Conquistadors
Rationale

Before investigating the consequences of the Spanish encounter with the Aztec civilisation, it is worth exploring the circumstances of the meeting and the motives of the Spanish. The latter are often described as *conquistadors*, a word which has connotations of conquest, exploration and adventure. The motives of the Spanish can be summed by three words used by Columbus to summarise his ambitions when setting out on his voyages of discovery: 'God, Gold and Cathay'. As devout Catholics, the Spanish felt compelled to spread their religion to the peoples of the new lands that had been discovered by Columbus. In doing so, they hoped to find a route to China (for which 'Cathay' is an ancient term) and consequently great wealth through increased trade. Whilst exploring the islands of the Caribbean, Spanish explorers began to hear rumours and stories about an immensely wealthy civilisation on the mainland of Central America and the prospect of gold and great riches began to seem closer at hand than distant China. The Spanish, therefore, had potentially conflicting motives for their actions and the results of these conflicts can be seen in the events that followed the fateful meeting between the conquistadors and the Aztecs in 1519.

Activity

Begin by outlining the circumstances of the Spanish expedition to the mainland of Central America in 1519. After the discovery of the islands of the West Indies by Columbus in 1492, King Charles V of Spain sent expeditions to establish settlements. Among the settlers was a 30 year-old, failed law student named Hernan Cortes. He proved himself to be an able soldier and became governor of the Spanish colony on the island of Cuba. But the settlement was not a success, because the settlers succumbed to local diseases. Rumours of great cities and great wealth to the west on the mainland of Central America led the Spanish to prepare an expedition, with Cortes as its leader. He set off in March 1519 to find these cities and establish a colony.

Explain the scenario for a diamond ranking activity – see *Photocopiable 5* – which sorts nine statement cards into a diamond shape from most to least relevant, each card giving a reason that a Spanish conquistador might have joined Cortes's expedition from Cuba to the mainland of Central America.

■ Activity 4 – Encountering the Aztecs
Rationale

The encounter between the Spanish and the Aztecs is one of the most significant in history, in that it defined the fate of an entire continent (North and South America) for hundreds of years afterwards, providing a template for conquest and exploitation of Native American peoples by several colonial European powers, including the British in North America. At the centre of the story is the unwitting spread of European diseases to America that fatally weakened native populations, making it possible for small numbers of Spanish conquistadors to subjugate entire civilisations, such as the Aztecs and later the Incas in Peru. In the case of the encounter with the Aztecs, the Spanish numbered no more than 600 soldiers (with less than twenty horses), led by Hernan Cortes. Montezuma, the Aztec leader (or Great Speaker) in 1519, initially assumed Cortes was Quetzalcoatl – a returning God-King.

Activity

The events that followed Cortes's arrival in Mexico are documented in several sources. Cortes himself wrote several letters to the Spanish king describing Tenochtitlan and his meetings with Montezuma. Bernal Diaz, who was a soldier at the time, later produced *The True History of the Conquest of New Spain* (1568), presenting the perspective of a conquistador. Aztec perspectives were recorded by sympathetic priests, such as Diego Duran (*The History of the Indies of New Spain* 1581) and Bernardino de Sahagún (*The Florentine Codex* 1540). The rapid conquest and subjugation of the Mexican people by the Spanish is clearly evident from all the sources, but the reasons for Spanish success, the motivations of participants and the precise sequence of events vary greatly across the range of sources.

Divide the children into two groups, representing the Spanish and the Aztecs. Provide each group with the extracts from sources on *Photocopiables 6 – 10* cut up onto separate cards: make sure the Spanish group see only the cards on *Photocopiables 6, 8* and *9* and the Aztecs only cards on Photocopiables 7 and 10. Point out that, although the

Spanish were fewer in number than the Aztecs, we have more extracts from the Spanish side: can the children suggest why this is so?

Depending on children's experience in interpreting sources, you can give out only limited numbers of the cards and present them sequentially to help in conveying the story of the encounter. Get the Spanish and the Aztec groups to work in teams to produce newspaper-style accounts of the events following Cortes's arrival on the coast of Mexico, eg for *The Spanish Sun* and *The Aztec Times*. The story is in three distinct stages – events on the coast, the Spanish journey to Tenochtitlan and the events in Tenochtitlan which led to Aztec rebellion and defeat. Either using all the cards or smaller sets, encourage the children to identify a chronological order of events. Note that nearly all the cards are extracts from primary sources, with slight simplification of language; only the final card on *Photocopiable 6* is an amalgamation of several Spanish sources.

After the children have constructed their distinct Spanish and Aztec versions of events, through discussion in a plenary, get the two groups to identify key events about which both sides can agree, e.g. the friendly welcome by the Aztecs on the coast, the human sacrifice witnessed by the Spanish on the way to Tenochtitlan and the significance of smallpox to the success of the Spanish conquest. Emphasise that an historian's role is to interpret potentially conflicting sources (ie from Spanish and Aztec perspectives), to try to identify the truth of what occurred.

Photocopiable 4 – Evidence Recording Sheet

Food	Dress/Clothes
Music	**Recreation**
Art	**Language**
Religion	**Rulers**

Photocopiable 5 – Motives of a Spanish Conquistador

A	B
You are a soldier, so you want to fight in battles.	You want to take your Christian religion to the people of the lands you discover.
C	**D**
You have heard stories about a City of Gold called El Dorado and you want to see if the story is true.	You want to find gold and jewellery so that you can return to Spain as a rich man.
E	**F**
You want to find new lands and become famous as an explorer.	You want to learn the languages spoken by the people you discover.
G	**H**
You want to get away from Cuba because it is not a healthy place to live.	You think that Hernan Cortes is a great leader and will follow him anywhere.
I	
You want to find a route to China, so you can bring back cloth and spices to Spain.	

Diamond Ranking

Most important relevant motive ⟶

Least important/relevant motive ⟶

Photocopiable 6 – Cortes arrives in Mexico: Spanish View
from the *The True History of the Conquest of New Spain* by Bernal Diaz (1568)

On Holy Thursday in the year 1519, we arrived with all the fleet. The flagship hoisted her royal standards and flags, and within half an hour of anchoring, two large canoes came out to us, full of Mexican Indians. They went direct to the flagship and going on board asked who was the *Tatuan*, which in their language means the chief. Then the Indians paid many marks of respect to Cortes and bade him welcome, and said that their lord, the great Montezuma, had sent them to ask what kind of men we were and of what we were in search, and added that if we were in need of anything for ourselves or the ships, that we should tell them and they would supply it.

Cortes thanked the Indians and ordered food and wine to be given them and some blue beads. After they had drunk he told them that we came to see them and to trade with them and that our arrival in their country should cause them no uneasiness but be looked on by them as fortunate. The messengers returned well content.

On Easter Sunday, the governor whom they spoke of arrived. His name was Tendile and he brought with him Pitalpitoque who was also a man of importance amongst the Indians and there followed many Indians with presents of fowls and vegetables.

With that Tendile took out a *petaca* – which is a sort of chest – many articles of gold and ordered ten loads of white cloth made of cotton and feathers to be brought, wonderful things to see, and there were other things which I do not remember, besides quantities of food consisting of fowls of the country, fruit and baked fish. Cortes received it all with smiles in a gracious manner and gave in return, beads of twisted glass and other small beads from Spain.

Tendile brought with him some clever painters such as they had in Mexico and ordered them to make pictures true to nature of the face and body of Cortes and all his captains, and of the soldiers, ships, sails and horses, so that they could be shown to his king, Montezuma.

Cortes ordered our gunners to load the cannons with a great charge of powder so that they should make a great noise when they were fired off, and he told Pedro de Alvarado that he and all the horsemen should get ready so that these servants of Montezuma might see them gallop. The cannons were fired off, and as it was quite still at that moment, the stones went flying through the forest with a great noise. The Indians were frightened by things so new to them, and ordered the painters to record them so that Montezuma might see.

Photocopiable 7 – Cortes arrives in Mexico: Aztec View

From *The History of the Indies of New Spain* by Diego Duran (1581) and The Florentine Codex by Bernardino de Sahagún (1540)

Montezuma told his messengers: 'I wish you to carry jewels and featherwork as presents to those who have arrived in our land. I want you to find out who their chieftain is. You must discover if he is the one called Quetzalcoatl, the Feathered Serpent. Our histories tell that he left this land but said that one day he would return to rule over it. You must also give him all kinds of food. If, by any chance, he does not like the food and wishes to eat human beings, allow yourselves to be eaten. I promise that I will look after your wives and children.'

Montezuma's messengers went to the floating house of the strangers, amazed at its size and strength. The floating house seemed more a thing of the gods than something made by human beings. The messengers gave the jewels and featherwork to the strangers. When the strangers saw the gifts, they were filled with great joy.

Montezuma took the string of beads saying, 'I accept the gift which the god has given me.' He gave orders that the necklace be buried at the feet of the god Hummingbird, as he was not worthy to wear such a holy thing

---

They dress in metal and wear metal hats on their heads. Their swords are metal. Their bows are metal. Their shields are metal. Their spears are metal. The strangers' bodies are completely covered, so that only their faces can be seen. Their skin is white as if it were made of lime plaster. They have yellow hair, though some have black. Their beards are long and yellow, and their moustaches are also yellow. Their hair is curly, with very fine strands.

The thunder is deafening. A thing like a ball of stone comes out of its belly. It comes out shooting sparks and raining fire. The smoke smells horrible, like rotten mud. If it is aimed at a mountain, the mountain cracks open. If it is aimed at a tree, it shatters the tree to dust.'

Their deer carry them on their backs wherever they wish to go. These deer are as tall as the roof of a house. Their dogs are very big, with folded ears and long, dangling tongues. Their eyes are burning yellow and flash like fire. They are very powerful. They run here and there panting, and they are flecked like a jaguar.

Photocopiable 8 – On the way to Tenochtitlan: Spanish View
from the *The True History of the Conquest of New Spain* by Bernal Diaz (1568)

On the fourth day of our journey to Tenochtitlan, I entered a province called Xicochimalco. This land is in the kingdom of Montezuma. Here they welcomed me and generously gave me the food I needed for the journey. (Cortes)

Beyond Xicochimalco, we crossed a pass over some high mountains and entered uninhabited country, where it was very cold and where it rained and hailed. That night we were very short of food, and a wind blew off the snowy heights which made us shiver.

Each day, the Cempoalans sacrificed before our eyes four or five Indians, whose hearts were offered to their idols and whose blood was plastered on the walls. Cortes told them that if they gave up this wicked practice, not only would we be their friends, but also we would give them other lands to rule. The chiefs and priests replied that it would be wrong for them to give up their idols and their sacrifices, for these gods of theirs brought them health and good harvests and all they needed.

Cortes told us that we must overthrow the idols that very day, and be ready to fight if they tried to stop us. Some fifty of us soldiers climbed up and overturned the idols, which rolled down the steps and were smashed to pieces. When they saw their idols were shattered, the Cempoalans wept and covered their eyes.

They strike open the poor Indian's chest with flint knives and quickly tear out the throbbing heart, which, with the blood, they present to the idols of their gods. Then they cut off the arms, thighs, and head, eating the arms and thighs at their religious feasts.'

We followed the causeway which goes straight to the city of Tenochtitlan. Wide though the causeway was, it was so crowded with people that we could hardly get through. No wonder, since they had never seen horses or men like us before! With such wonderful sights to gaze on we did not know what to say, or if what we saw was real. On the lake side there were great cities, and on the lake many more, and before us was the great city of Tenochtitlan.

As for us, we were scarcely 400 strong, and we well remembered the many warnings we had received to beware of entering the city of Tenochtitlan, since they would kill us as soon as they had us inside. What men in all the world have shown such daring?

Photocopiable 9 – Cortes in Tenochtitlan: Spanish View
from the *The True History of the Conquest of New Spain* by Bernal Diaz (1568)

The great Montezuma was about forty years old, of good height, well shaped and slim. His skin was not very dark, though of the usual Indian complexion. He did not wear his hair long, but just over his ears. He could be warm and friendly, but when necessary, he was very serious. He was very neat and clean, and took a bath every afternoon. The clothes he wore one day he did not wear again till three or four days later.

Only some of his chieftains were allowed to speak to him and when they came before him they had to take off their rich cloaks and walk barefoot. The lords had to look downwards, for they were not allowed to look him in the face. As they went out they did not turn their backs on him, but kept their faces towards him and their eyes downcast, only turning round when they had left the room.

One day Cortes said to Montezuma: 'In going about your father's palace these Christians have discovered a certain amount of gold and taken it. Do not be angry about it.'

Moctezuma answered; 'That treasure belongs to the gods of our people. Take the gold, but leave the things like featherwork and other pieces that are not gold. I shall give you all the gold that I have. For you must know that from the beginning of time we have believed that the people who used to rule this land came from a faraway place and that they came in ships and then went away again. They said they would return, and we have always believed that some time they would come to rule and command us. Our gods and priests have always promised it would happen and now it has come about.'

On learning that the Indians had attacked his soldiers on the coast, Cortes told his captains to come along with him, with some soldiers, to Montezuma's palace. When they had entered the palace, Cortes politely asked Montezuma to go with him to the Spaniards' quarters so that he would not be harmed. Montezuma refused, replying that the captain had no reason for taking him as a captive, after he had welcomed us so well and given his loyalty to the Spanish King. Then Cortes said to him: 'You must go with us because you have waged war against the Christians I left at the sea port.' Montezuma answered angrily that he had ordered no such thing.

When the Indians rebelled against us, we were outnumbered, but God saw fit to send smallpox to weaken the Indians. Cortes had boats built with cannons to attack the city from the lake. With many Indians on our side, those called Aztecs were beaten by our weapons, by hunger and by disease.

Photocopiable 10 – Cortes in Tenochtitlan: Aztec View

from *The History of the Indies of New Spain* by Diego Duran (1581) and The Florentine Codex by Bernardino de Sahagún (1540)

When the strangers were settled in the palace, they asked Montezuma about the city's wealth. They questioned him closely and demanded gold. Montezuma took them to the Treasure House. When they arrived at the Treasure House, the riches of gold and feathers were brought out to them: feathers, decorated shields, discs of gold and gold ornaments.

The strangers stripped the feathers from the gold shields and standards. They gathered all the gold into a pile and set fire to everything else, no matter its value. Then they melted the gold down. As for the green stones, they took only the best – the Tlaxcalans snatched the rest up. Next the strangers searched through Montezuma's personal treasure store. They grinned like little beasts and patted each other with delight

The strangers did many cruel deeds on the way to Tenochtitlan. One took place in Cholula, and it was a sorry affair. There, in the courtyard of the temple where the strangers were staying, they killed a great number of men who had come along to serve them. These people had carried water, firewood and grass for the horses.

The strangers burst into smiles. Their eyes gleamed. They were delighted by these gifts. They picked up the gold – they picked it up like monkeys. The truth is, they longed and lusted for gold. Their bodies swelled with their greed – they were hungry like pigs for that gold.

They came dressed for battle to overcome us, and the dust rose in whirlwinds on the roads. Their spears glinted in the sun, and their long-tailed flags fluttered like bats. They made a loud noise as they marched, for their metal armour and their weapons clashed and rattled. Some were dressed in shining metal from head to foot. They terrified everyone.

The Spaniards murdered the Aztecs who were celebrating the Fiesta of Huitzilopochtli in the place they called The Patio of the Gods. When everyone was enjoying the fiesta, when everyone was already dancing, when everyone was already singing, in that precise moment the Spaniards decided to kill people. They came armed for battle.

When people outside learned of the massacre, shouting began, 'Captains, Mexicas, come here quickly! Come here with all arms, spears, and shields! Our people have been murdered!' Then a roar was heard, screams, people wailed, as they beat their palms against their lips. Quickly the captains assembled and carried their spears and shields. Then the battle began. We attacked them with arrows and even spears, including small spears used for hunting birds.

Broken spears lie on the roads. We have torn our hair in grief. Our houses have no roofs, their walls are red with blood. The water has turned red and has a bitter taste. We have chewed dry twigs, we have filled our mouths with dust, we have eaten lizards, rats and worms. We beat our hands in despair against the walls. For our city is lost and dead. Weep, weep our people, for we have lost Tenochtitlan. The shields of our warriors could not save it.

Resources

Several good quality, non-fiction books for children are available about the Aztecs and the encounter with the Spanish, including:

■ Baquedano E (2006) *Eyewitness Guide: Aztec.* Dorling Kindersley

■ Macdonald F (1993) *Insights: The Aztecs.* Barrons

■ Malam A (2003) *Exploring the Aztecs (Remains to Be Seen).* Evans

■ Rees R (2006) *The Aztecs (Understanding People in the Past).* Heinemann Library

■ Triggs T (2005) *Primary History: Aztecs.* Folens

Web resources about the Aztecs are plentiful, but only a few are really suitable for independent research by children. These include:

■ *Snaith Primary School Aztecs* – http://home.freeuk.net/elloughton13/aztecs.htm

■ *Nettlesworth Primary School Aztecs* – www.nettlesworth.durham.sch.uk/time/aztec.html

■ *Learning Connections Aztecs Primary Project* – www.learning-connections.co.uk/ curric/cur_pri/aztecs

■ *ThinkQuest The Ancient Aztecs* – http://library.thinkquest.org/27981

■ *The Aztec Calendar* – www.azteccalendar.com

Chapter 8

Religious Education and the global dimension

Carol Fry

Rationale

By definition, Religious Education is a subject which always involves global issues. It is about people and the values and beliefs which determine their lifestyles. It involves the study of the six major religions of the world (Buddhism, Christianity, Hinduism, Islam, Judaism and Sikhism) both in relation to their representation in Britain today, and to the cultures from which they arise.

The Non-Statutory National Framework for RE (2004) describes the two Attainment Targets for Religious Education in the following terms:

Learning about religion includes enquiry into, and investigation of, the nature of religion. It focuses on beliefs, teachings and sources, practices and ways of life and forms of expression. It includes the skills of interpretation, analysis and explanation. Pupils learn to communicate their knowledge and understanding using specialist vocabulary. It includes identifying and developing an understanding of ultimate questions and ethical issues.

Learning from religion is concerned with developing pupils' reflection on, and response to, their own experiences and learning about religion. It develops pupils' skills of application, interpretation and evaluation of what they learn about religion, particularly questions of identity and belonging, meaning, purpose, truth, values and commitments, and communicating their responses.' (QCA, 2004)

Although school programmes for Religious Education are determined by the locally agreed syllabus of the Local Authority, Attainment Targets for the subject are increasingly close to those of the National Framework, and reflect the same ideas, albeit sometimes in different language. Both these Attainment Targets require pupils to look beyond themselves and their immediate world, and to enter into the worldview of others, looking at beliefs, values and practices. They both also involve pupils thinking about the big questions of life, which necessarily include such issues as justice and injustice, poverty, suffering and the 'why?' questions with which all human beings, including children, are faced.

Religious Education is thus essentially about diversity. It is also about challenging stereotypes. It requires children to think beyond immediate appearances and to consider deeper questions. Even if the main content of religious education were to be about Christianity, it should never be about presenting Christianity in Anglo-centric or even Anglican-centric terms. It needs always to be about the recognition of diversity, and the idea that members of any faith come in many shapes and forms. This approach is well demonstrated in many of the commercially produced schemes for religious education. Within a class, except in faith schools, the majority of children are likely to come from non-religious backgrounds. Of those who come from a religious background, many will be from Muslim, Sikh or Hindu heritages, as well as some Christians. Yet often the Religious Education which is taught presumes familiarity with the practice of the local Anglican church, when those children who are church-going are more likely to be from Baptist churches, or from charismatic, independent churches. In addition, there may be children who are new arrivals from Eastern Europe, and who represent the current resurgence of Catholicism or Eastern forms of Christianity.

The same principles of diversity should apply whatever religion we are discussing. Teachers often talk about the problems of representing the breadth of denominational diversity within Christianity, or of representing both Orthodox and Progressive Judaism, and fear that to try to represent all faiths will confuse the children. This is true, but it is equally wrong to try to reduce a religion or tradition to its lowest common denominator which may be unrecognisable to members of the faith community concerned. This is where words like 'most'; 'many' and 'some' are particularly helpful for teachers. By saying 'many Christians do ... many Jews do ... some Hindus believe ...' does not exclude the

experience of those who belong to different traditions within a faith, where there are different forms of practice, or where different cultural influences are at work. More fundamentally, it is helpful in this context to be aware of the ethnographic approach to the study of religion and of Religious Education. This is best represented by the work of Professor Robert Jackson and his team at the University of Warwick. Their work has been based on longitudinal studies of children growing up in the midlands, and of the effects of the diversity of cultures to which they belong. The approaches of this project are reflected in their published materials for primary schools, *Bridges to Religions* (see Resources). Whilst these publications focus on the lives of children living in Britain, they embed the global principle by their strong focus on the diversity of backgrounds and cultures from which the children in their materials come.

Activities
Key Stage One

Precious
Outline planning for a sequence of lessons for Reception/Y1
The topic of Precious is one which is frequently employed in Key Stage One Religious Education. It gives pupils some important foundational experiences, whilst at the same time allowing them to begin to explore important concepts such as the sacred, and sacred objects and places. It also allows children to begin to recognise that different people have different needs and values and that different things are precious to different people. Objectives for Key Stage One are shown. The planning will also develop skills, knowledge and understandings in relevant Areas of Learning from the Early Years Foundation Stage.

Objectives Learning *By the end of the activity pupils will be able to ...*	Content	Resources	Assessment for *Can a pupil ... ?*
1. Express their ideas orally (AT2 L1) 2. Reflect on what is of importance to them (AT 2 L1/2) 3. Recognise things which are of importance to others (AT2 L1/2)	**What is precious to us?** 1 Before the lesson -ask the children to bring in something which is precious to them (make sure that parents understand the nature of what is being asked for) 2 Teacher to bring in some objects of different sorts, including probably an old teddy bear, or some other battered but well loved toy 3 Children and teachers to talk about these precious things and why they are precious to them 4 Set up a display, and write about /draw our precious things 5 Get children to begin to think about why things are precious (e.g. 'it reminds me of ...', 'x gave it to me', 'I've had it since I was a baby' etc. NB Since many of these precious things will have to go home that day, you could take digital pictures of some to use on the interactive whiteboard in later lessons	Precious items brought in Digital camera	1. Express his/her ideas orally 2. Recognise and respect the precious things of other people 3. Explain why some things are precious to people

Objectives Learning By the end of the activity pupils will be able to ...	Content	Resources	Assessment for Can a pupil ... ?
1. Describe the ways in which we look after precious things (AT2 L1) 2. Describe some religious artefacts (AT1 L1) 3. Relate these artefacts to their use(AT1 L1/2) 4. Recognise these as precious or 'sacred' objects and understand how these should be treated. (AT 1 L1/2)	**How do we look after precious things? / What is precious to other people (2 lessons)** 1 Thinking again about the precious things – provide reminders through images shared with the whole class. 2 How do we look after them? Where do we keep them? How would we feel if anything happened to them? What makes our precious things different from someone else's? 3 Introduce some items, which are precious to particular groups of people, and are used within the home. Depending on the religions which have been studied, these may be, for instance, some Shabbat items from Judaism, or some Hindu murtis 4 Allow children to explore and draw these items, but be sensitive to what they should handle. Understanding that they should not handle certain items is part of their learning within this topic 5 Explain to children the ideas of preciousness or specialness of these items and explain their use within the home – some simple video/DVD clips, or pictures would be helpful here.	Images Religious artefacts Reconstructions of artefacts or play versions' of certain artefacts. Short DVD extracts of artefacts in their context.	1. Describe how we look after precious things. 2. Correctly identify some religious artefacts and relate them to their context 3. Show sensitivity and respect in the handling of artefacts

Objectives Learning By the end of the activity pupils will be able to ...	Content	Resources	Assessment for Can a pupil ... ?
1 Explain ways in which aspects of the natural world are precious (AT2 L1/2) 2 Recognise the limitations of natural resources (AT2 L1) 3 Show understanding of the needs of others.(AT2 L1)	**What else is precious?** 1. Have resources set up ready with items such as a jug of water, some basic foods, pictures of the natural environment 2. Talk about water. To whom is this precious? Why is it precious? Get children to suggest the range of uses. What would it be like if they didn't have water? Tell stories of children in areas of poverty or drought 3. A similar activity can be undertaken with food. Think about people who do not just go to the supermarket or local shop, but who have to go to the markets and queue for very limited resources. (Be careful here about stereotypes of less economically developed localities) Depending on the age of the children, may also consider sensitively the situation of those who are dependent on food aid	Water, foods, pictures Materials form Christian Aid, CAFOD, Tearfund or Water Aid. There are many simple stories from these sources on children and their daily experience.	1 Describe the ways in which they use natural resources 2 Identify a range of things which they take for granted which children in the developing world may not have
1 Compare some of the different ways in which things are 'precious' 2 Suggest reasons why these different things are all regarded as precious 3 Some will be able to make links between values and commitments and attitudes and behaviour (AT2 L3)	**Review** 1 Remind children of the different kinds of precious things which have been considered previously 2 Get children to think about the range of precious things, and draw/write/talk about these 3 Ask them to suggest why all count as precious, and why. This is a hard question but should encourage them to think about ideas of what is really important, or really special in people's lives	Materials from previous lessons	1 Give a range of possible meanings of 'precious' and suggest connections between them

Key Stage Two
Christianity as a world religion – teaching about Christianity and enhancing the global dimension

Background to the Key Stage Two activities

It is often the case when teaching Religious Education, that teachers tend to talk about Christianity in comparison to world religions, with the latter being characterised as the faiths of other cultures. This carries with it a lot of assumptions, and is a potential source of misconception for children. Christianity is a world religion and this concept should underpin much of what is done in Key Stage Two and throughout the primary school. We should ask the same questions of Christianity as we do of any other religion – for example, 'Who are these people?', 'What do they do?', 'How do they worship?', and so on. It is often the case that although there may be little real knowledge of Christianity among pupils, there is an assumed familiarity. It may be that children have to pass several churches, or former churches, on their way to school, without ever being challenged to ask what they are, or what goes on within them. The school terms are still mainly organised around the times of Christian festivals, and children's Religious Education will certainly contain reference to Christmas and Easter, even if they have little knowledge of the doctrines or practices associated with these festivals. Although there may be more cultural familiarity, the same questions and the same methods of study need to be asked of Christianity as of any other religion.

Christianity is a global phenomenon. This does not just relate to geographical distribution but more especially to the variety of cultural forms, which it may take. However, many adults contribute to misconceptions in this respect. For example, many children, and indeed adults, make the assumption that Christianity is a religion of white people. Although statistics are variable, it may be that worldwide Christianity is now a predominantly black and Asian religion. The shift in the centre of gravity of Christianity has been commented on by, among others, Samuel Kobia, the General Secretary of the World Council

of Churches in 2005. His comments relate to the geographical distribution of Christianity. There are many thousands of black and Asian Christians in Europe and North America and representations of Christianity often lack a European dimension. How many children have even heard of Lutheranism, the Christian tradition dominant in Germany and Scandinavia?

Against this background, the following principles may be employed with in any plans or schemes of work on Christianity:

- What range of denominational traditions are we reflecting?

- What range of cultural backgrounds are we reflecting

- Has the selection, which we have made, truly represented the faith concerned?

The suggestions which follow are based on picture activities, which involve the skills of empathy and interpretation, as well as developing some thinking skills.

Activities

Since all Agreed Syllabi require a strong focus on Christianity, and some faith schools will be teaching to Diocesan syllabi which allow an even stronger focus on Christianity, the two examples below are both taken from that faith to exemplify a principle and a methodology. In different ways, the same principles could be employed for several religions. For instance, the picturing Jesus activities could also be used for teaching about the Buddha, and the work on churches could be applied to the study of the places of worship of any religion.

Jesus

The activity is based on children looking at and responding to pictures of Jesus. The pictures need to include some classics of renaissance art as well as modern western images and some from African and Asian sources. Images can easily be sourced from Art books as well as from downloaded images.

Give pairs or groups of children different pictures, and ask them to interrogate these, or perhaps list a series of questions about the picture or the event it portrays. They could think of a name for the picture, and formulate a list of things they notice about it. They might also try to suggest why the artist included certain features. In the discussion which follows some children may respond negatively to images of Jesus as a black or Asian figure. This gives good opportunities to challenge stereotypes, and to encourage pupils to think about Christians from a variety of races and cultures. If asked which picture they think best represents Jesus, they are likely to choose one of the classics of western art. A discussion on this should take them to three main teaching points:

- that no-one knows what Jesus looked like

- whatever he looked like, he was middle eastern and not European, so the African and Asian pictures are no more wrong than are the Northern European ones

- that people perceive and represent Jesus, or other leaders, in terms of their own culture and way of life

In undertaking this activity, children are being introduced to the global dimension in a variety of forms. Their thinking about Christianity is being challenged, and they are also being introduced to artistic styles they are not familiar with, and this may also challenge their thinking.

This work could lead to further work on some of the stories depicted, or it could lead to work on festivals (if the pictures relate to Christmas, Easter or Pentecost) Alternatively, for more able pupils, it can lead to some deeper learning, based on the idea of interpretation. What were these artists trying to say – Who was Jesus? (AT 1 L3/4, AT2 L3).

Churches

This is another picture-based activity which can be used with a variety of age groups, and is easy to resource. All that is needed is a large variety of pictures of Christian churches, exteriors or interiors – preferably both. Try to make sure that the images include for example,

- some old country churches

- some modern urban churches from various parts of the world

- some plain and simple buildings

- some Eastern Orthodox churches, especially Russian

- Black-led churches in Britain

- some Indian or African churches

Ask friends to send pictures of churches rather than beaches for their holiday postcards and this topic will soon be resourced. Again, pictures can easily be accessed from the Web; it is important to print these out, as this makes pupil selection and group discussion easier. If using digital images, it is useful to have them on the computer for projection on an interactive whiteboard or large screen, so that in discussion all pupils can focus on the same picture and detail can be highlighted.

Display the pictures on the wall, or spread them on a table. Ask the pupils each to choose one they particularly like and one they particularly dislike and to think about the reasons why. This initial stage is best done quietly and individually, so that personal responses can be given. Whenever this activity is done, all children have an opinion: it makes little difference whether or not they have any personal experience of going into a Christian church.

Encourage the children to discuss their ideas and preferences. Ask some children to talk about their particular likes and dislikes and to give their reasons. At this stage it would be helpful to project some of the images so that all children can see the details and all can focus on the same image. The usual responses to this activity are that children like little country churches because they look cosy, quiet, peaceful or spooky. The chocolate box images often top the popularity poll! This may be because they look like the pupils' standard images of churches: children often dislike more modern buildings or those from unfamiliar cultures.

This can then lead into discussion of questions such as:

- Why are these buildings different from each other?

- Where are they located? Does this make a difference to the appearance of the buildings?

- Can you guess where they might be? What clues are there?

- How old are the buildings?

- What goes on inside them? Does this make a difference to the sorts of building that they are? This helps children to think about diversity and denominational difference. If there are pictures of interiors and exteriors, get the children to try to relate them to each other.

- If looking at pictures of worship taking place inside the building, ask children to think about where the building might be. This would be particularly useful when looking at worship by a predominantly black congregation in a Pentecostal church in Britain: children may suggest that this is an African country or the West Indies. Helping them to realise that this may be a church not far from them can begin to break down stereotypes of Christianity as a white religion.

- Does a church have to look like a church? What sorts of images are appropriate in the 21st century? A simple activity is to get the children to imagine that a church is to be built in a new housing development in their locality, and to suggest the form that it might take. If emphasising the global dimension, it is appropriate to ask the same question about a contrasting locality which they have been studying. (AT 1 L3/4. Some may pursue questions to access L5. AT2 L3/4)

Resources

Books

Blaylock, L. (2001) *Picturing Jesus.* Birmingham: Christian Education Publications

Cooling, M. (1998) *Jesus Through Art.* Exeter: RMEP

Grimmitt, M, Grove, J, Hull, J and Spencer, L. (1991) *A Gift to the Child.* Cheltenham: Nelson Thornes

Grimmitt, M, Hull, JM, Tellam, L, Grove, J and Grove, E. (2006) *A Gift to the Child (Series2).* Bury: Articles of Faith.

Jackson, R. (1997) *RE an Interpretive Approach.* London, Hodder Murray

Jackson, R, Barratt, M, and Etherington, J. (1994) *Bridges to Religions* (Teachers' Book).Oxford: Heinemann

Wood, A. (1998) *Homing in.* Stoke on Trent: Trentham Books

Websites

Stories and other materials for use in the third Key Stage One activity are available from the following sources:

- *Christian Aid* – www.christianaid.org.uk

- *CAFOD* – www.cafod.org.uk

- *Tearfund* – www.tearfund.org

- *Water Aid* – www.wateraid.org.uk

Religious artefacts (including play versions) are available from

- *Articles of Faith,* Kay St, Bury BL9 6BU. Tel: 0161 763 6232. www.articlesoffaith.co.uk

- *Religion in Evidence,* TTS Group Ltd, Park Lane Business Park, Kirkby-in-Ashfield, Nottinghamshire, NG17 9LE. Tel: 0800 318 686 www.tts-group.co.uk

Chapter 9

Drama and the global dimension

Allan Owens

Rationale

For primary teachers using drama activities, the global dimension encourages them to consider how effective their use of drama is in enabling children and those working with them to not only read the word, but to 'read the world' (Freire, 1990). This involves imaginative enquiry into their own identities, families, communities, disability, being a girl or a boy, theirs and others' cultural and ethnic groups, similarities and differences and about personal, local and global power relationships.

This focus is markedly different from that of twenty years ago in the UK when much drama and arts work operated on a reading of multiculturalism that often privileged the celebration of other peoples and cultures as an end in itself. The shift has been from a multicultural arts celebration of diversity to the intercultural acknowledgement that 'every group counts', without ducking 'the hard issues of negative perceptions, intolerance and prejudice' (Knowles and Ridley, 2006). Drama and arts education practice in the UK has always espoused the principles of respect and tolerance that underpin all global dimension documentation but now they are very much about identifying, reflecting on and challenging attitudes to groups who are perceived as different, and about developing our ability to question what we have learned or been told about the out-group.

This does not mean that play, enjoyment and imaginative engagement are lost, but that the learning about the world and the action we can take in it are made explicit. The western dramatic tradition has always been concerned with the action individuals and communities can take, what agency we have, in the face of the structures we confront. This can be traced back to Greek theatre, through to Shakespeare, Brecht and contemporary playwrights, such as Edward Bond. The global dimension of drama in the curriculum is about enabling participants to ask the difficult questions about what it might mean to be or not to be accepted in a society; to consider the actions that might be taken if we believe we really can influence global issues. The central idea is that drama can play a similar role in the community of the school as it does in the life of society – by representing, commenting on and inviting discussion about the issues and concerns that affect our community, life and the world that we share and which our children will inherit (Dickenson and Neelands, 2006).

Primary schools use a wide range of drama activities for a variety of purposes that inform and are informed by the global dimension. These include: role play, games, improvised scenes, theatre-in-education, forum theatre, process drama, mantle of the expert, play reading, class or school performances, visiting artist projects, theatre, museum and gallery trips. The focus of this chapter is process drama, because its clear story lines and dilemmas make it a readily accessible drama activity. References for drama activities are at the end of the chapter.

The two key examples of drama practice presented here arise from collaborative work with primary school colleagues in the UK and Palestine. The situation concerning Palestine and Israel is controversial, particularly in terms of human rights issues. I have chosen to focus on this contested situation to demonstrate how drama can enable children, teachers and other participants to engage deeply but safely with controversial issues. Those who know little about this specific situation may be motivated to find out more and can take the opportunity to make connections with other controversial issues that are familiar.

First we'll look at a ready-to-use process drama that can enrich and inform the curriculum in ways that not only meet, but transcend, the National Curriculum requirements for Drama within the Standing Orders of English, Speaking and Listening for Key Stages one and two

pupils to make, perform and respond to a wide range of drama activities (DfES, 1999).

Activities
Key Stage One

Three Friends

This drama is based on a traditional Palestinian story and I thank Hamdeh Baalosha, from the Gaza Drama Project Group, for sharing it with me. At its simplest the drama is about the nature of friendship and inclusion. Used in a cross-curricular setting it can be a doorway to explore concepts of diversity, difference, interdependence and sustainable development. The drama is in three parts that could run over half a term or provide the focus for a global dimension day or week.

Activity

Tell the children 'The drama we are going to work on together is about three animals. The first moves very fast. Ask, 'What is this animal?' Come to an agreement. (The fastest is the cheetah, capable of travelling at a burst of speed of 70 miles per hour.)

Ask the children 'What letter does the animal's name start with?' – for example, C, if Cheetah. Then ask, 'What first name starts with this letter?' For example, 'Charlotte Cheetah'.

Ask, 'What is the second animal in this story, the slowest animal?' (The three-toed sloth is one of the slowest, capable of travelling three metres a minute or 90 metres per hour.)

Ask the class to name the animal as in step 2, for example S for Shelley, if a Snail.

Ask, 'What is the third animal in this drama?' It moves at a speed some where between the fastest and the slowest. Repeat the naming process.

Tell the class, 'This drama is based on a story from Palestine. It is about animals, but it is also a metaphor that allows us to make connections with our own lives and those of others.'

Start narrating. 'There were once three unlikely, but very good friends (use the names and animals they have given). Our drama starts on their first day at school.'

Next share information or shift the activity to information gathering or sorting on schooling around the world. For example, children start school at different ages in different countries: in Finland at seven, in Palestine at six. In Japan, some children this age travel to school squashed with friends on busy trains. In Sweden some walk to school alone along quiet forest roads. In Palestine and Israel some children pass patrols of soldiers on their way to school. In the UK, some parents drive their ten year-olds to school. In this drama we will begin to find out things about the society the three friends live in, as we make things up and look them up together. As we do this we can think about where we live; the similarities and differences.

Ask, 'What age shall we make the three friends in this drama?'

Continue the narration. 'Our drama starts on a very important day for the three friends: their first day at school. All started well when they set off.'

Ask, 'What time does school start for the animals?' Share information, for example in the UK it usually starts around 8:45am. In some countries, such as Palestine, there are two or three sittings in school and so school could start at 7.00am or 11.00am or 3.00pm.

Continue. 'All started well when they set off one hour before school, but with just fifteen minutes left they still had a long way to go. Shelley [slowest animal] was trying her best, but had hardly moved. The head teacher stood at the entrance to the school greeting the children on their first day. '

Ask, 'What sort of animal was the head teacher?' Agree on this.

Continue. 'Only three animals had not arrived. Far away, the three friends had an amazing idea about how they could all get to school on time.

Ask 'What was the amazing idea the three friends had to get to school on time?' Encourage the children to use their imagination. The solution does not have to be realistic; it can be fantastic. For example, the two friends could tie some elastic-type creeper between two trees to make a gigantic catapult and fire Shelley through the air in an arc. They could then run very fast in a straight line and be at the school in time to catch her!

Continue: 'Get into groups of four and devise a piece of drama that shows how the three friends solve the problem. The fourth member of the group is the narrator who tells the story as it is acted out. The solution must be no longer than one minute long and needs rehearsing before it is performed.'

Stop the groups after the allotted time and give them one more chance to run through with the narrator.

Take on the role of the head teacher of the animals' school and repeat the last part of the narration.

Get the class to watch each performance.

Reflect on the drama. For example: consider issues of diversity, interdependence, similarities and differences; respect; the right to go or not go to school. For example, a taxi might or might not be provided in the UK for a pupil in a wheelchair to get to school. In some cases and some countries there would be no choice but to set out early with the support of friends or family to get there and back. This can also be undertaken as an enquiry where the children's task could be to find out how many children in the world do not go to primary school and why. For example, 80 million children in the world don't get the chance to go to school and this is true of one in three girls in Ethiopia.

Thank the group for their work and as a way of introducing the second stage of the drama say 'We are beginning to find out a little more about the three friends. It is often in times of difficulty that we find out who our friends are, and who we are.'

Part one of this drama is tightly structured with a pre-determined focus. Part two allows the same initial structure to be used, but the teacher and the children can select the global dimension concept they want to focus on. The narrative centres on a problem faced a year later by the middle speed animal. The problem could be racist abuse and bullying by another animal when she walks the final part of the way home after school. She really cannot tell anyone what is happening. Worst of all she stole from her family because she was threatened. She is pretending to be ill. This scenario can be developed using the drama activities or strategies listed and referenced at the close of this chapter. In Part three the narrative focuses on a problem faced by the fastest animal and this could be handed over to the children. The teacher's work here is to discuss the focus, set initial boundaries and create challenges as needed.

Key Stage Two

Instead of looking at another ready-to-use drama, like *The Three Friends*, we'll turn to an example of drama being used to understand the nature of conflicts and controversial issues. This is based on a story called *The Slope* by Palestinian writer Ghassan Kanafani (1996). I would like to thank Suzan Al Rijai, from the South Hebron Drama Project Group for all her work on this drama. The structure uses a mixture of process drama and theatre-in-education strategies and requires the teacher and other adults to play roles within it – for the purposes of the description below, the other adults were a classroom assistant and a trainee teacher.

Activity

The class received a letter via the teacher from a person called Ali (trainee teacher) asking them if they could help with a difficult situation. Ali said that it would be helpful if the class and the teacher could learn some words in Arabic and Hebrew before meeting him in a week's time in the playground. I worked with the school to develop this project, but on the day I sat on the floor with the children as an observer. The following description is of the opening two prepared scenes in this interactive drama as I noted them down on the day.

Thirty children enter the classroom and gather around a woman (teacher-in-role), wearing a Palestinian shawl, who is repairing and making shoes. She looks up and says '*Marhaba*' ('Good morning' in Arabic) and that she is glad they have come. She tells about the small hut they are in where she works and lives. She also tells them about her employer: the man who she sends the shoes to each week in his big house overlooking her hut. She is plausible and likeable as she relates how she and her friends lost their homes when they were forced off the land to make room for the man and his friends. To make matters worse, he throws his orange peel down on her hut and it won't be long before she and the hut are buried. When the wind blows, the sand and earth pile up around the hut. Sometimes she gets no shoes to repair for weeks and so no money for food. This is her land, her home, but how can she carry on? She asks the children, 'Please, could you speak with that man. I believe he thinks that I am not a human being!'

The children ask questions and comment in the pauses she intentionally makes in the telling of her story such as,' Why are you mending shoes?', 'Why don't you go and get your home back?', 'How can you be buried under oranges?' They agree to help and Ali takes them to the man's house (the hall of the school).

When they meet the man (classroom assistant) he is busy sorting through business papers, eating oranges and throwing the peel over his shoulder. He welcomes them warmly and asks them to sit down. Before they get a chance to speak he tells them how badly he was treated in the land where he used to live; how cramped the boat was on which he left; how thrilled he was to come to this new land; how this hill was just a heap of earth with deserted huts on it before he arrived, a land in which nothing grew, but since he has built his house, irrigated the soil and planted orange groves things have got better. The people further down the slope have a chance to work and make something of their lives. As he talks with the children he is plausible and likeable, he tells how he has even given these people some land to live on. Instead of being grateful they are resentful, some of them have attacked homes higher up the slope and he is worried about violence.

As the man tells the children of his hopes and plans for the future, James, a seven year-old boy sidles up to me on the floor and whispers, 'How do we know who is telling the truth?'

James's question is at the heart of the drama. His teacher knows that this act of imaginative enquiry, of being someone else somewhere else in the present, past or future lies at the heart of drama in education. She often uses drama in line with Key Stage Two English, Speaking and Listening orders 'to explore the experiences of others'. She also knows that drama operates metaphorically as a means of exploring and illuminating life. The situation between the woman and the man is therefore 'like' and 'not like' the current situation in Israel and Palestine that they will look at later as an example of international conflict. The purpose of this form of drama activity is to prompt dialogue and critical reflection through reflections on the similarities and differences between an imaginary and real situation and the situation of the children's own lives. The intention behind this process is to challenge the children's, assistant's, parent's and teacher's values and perceptions as they engage with concepts of conflict resolution, human rights and social justice in the global dimension.

What has been set up is drama capable of operating on a powerful metaphorical level in a way that provides a safe doorway in to the controversial and contested situation in Palestine and Israel. The pupils are encouraged to identify with both characters in order to ask the difficult sort of question that James asked, 'Who is telling the truth?' As they move between the two characters they are encouraged by Ali to identify, narrate, consider and evaluate the different versions of the truth being told in the drama. In other words they assume 'a critical voice' (Britzman, 2003).

This does not mean that the struggles of others are devalued but that careful attention is paid to the tensions between and within the words they speak and the actions they take. Stories are set off in the drama, one against the other in order to allow the participants to question versions of 'the truth' being presented. Practised in this way, drama is a form of enquiry, useful for finding out what is going on in a particular place at a particular time. The task is to trace 'the circulation of competing regimes of truth' (Foucault, 1980). We are encouraged to ask: How did things come to be the way they are? How might we want them to be different?

Drama informed by the global dimension in this way involves creating an irresistible imaginative context to generate questions in the primary classroom. The questions motivate participants to search for materials and information, historical facts, figures and perspectives because their help is needed to provide answers, they are caught up in the felt human experience of the drama and want to understand more in order to help. The French philosopher, Paul Ricoeur argues that 'what is needed to understand is not instruction but imagination and intuition' (Simms, 2003). The emphasis on the use of the word 'understand' in this approach is not placed on 'pinning down the precise understanding derived from a particular drama' but on the 'constant process of redefining and deepening, seeing things from new angles, making fresh connections' (Fleming, 2001).

In *The Slope*, James and the class had the opportunity to extend their range of understanding about conflict resolution through direct experience of conflict between two people as they shuttled between them trying to find a solution. In questioning and challenging the perceptions and assumptions of these two roles, they were also reflecting on their own. For example, 'If you have been treated badly does that allow you to treat other people badly?' 'Does the person with the most power in a situation always win?' They experienced the difficulties in trying to get people to communicate, negotiate and compromise, for example in their attempt to stop the man throwing his orange peels over his shoulder. They saw close-up the impact of unequal power: the woman's lack of resources in stark contrast to the man's situation and the choices she and others like her have in conflict situations is negligible. They saw the exhaustion of the woman, the fear of the man and the need to help them and others involved to develop multiple perspectives in order to see events in new ways.

James and the class also got the chance to know about and reflect on different examples of conflict and their impact locally, nationally and internationally. For example, they questioned information about competing regimes of truth circulating around the Israel-Palestine situation such as the claim that the Palestinian narrative is heard less than Israel's in the British media. They looked at the map of Palestine, Israel and the Middle East with the teacher and reflected on how actions, choices and decisions taken in the UK can positively or negatively affect the quality of life of people in other countries.

They talked about the double promise made by the British to the Jewish community and the Palestinians. The promise to Jewish communities across Europe was that they could live in a new homeland called Israel that would be created in Palestine (originally proposed in the Balfour Declaration of 1917). The second promise was made to the Palestinians that their homeland would always be theirs. The children discussed the impossibility of fulfilling this double promise and the consequences of this for the children and adults of Palestine and Israel. The drama generated opportunities for this discussion and allowed those involved to 'critically examine their own values and attitudes; appreciate similarities between people everywhere, and value diversity; and develop skills that will enable them to combat injustice, prejudice and discrimination' (DfES, 2005, p.2).

Some other key uses of drama in the primary school

- To encourage play, including games and pretence in structured drama spaces where the teacher can intervene to deepen the play, such as in a role play area; with puppets and masks around tables; and in unstructured spaces which are often free from teacher intervention, such as the playground.

- Within a conventional lesson to enliven and enrich learning and teaching. For example, the use of drama conventions, such as hot seating, where a pupil takes on the role of an historical figure or character and improvises responses to questions from the rest of the class

- As a subject or themed focus in a specific curriculum area in the classroom and during the extended school day. For example, collaborative enquiry focused on geography, history and art in which the scripting, rehearsal and performance of plays is a central activity

- In collaboration with visiting artists as a pivotal whole year group or school event providing a shared experience and catalyst for high quality teaching and learning as part of a whole school approach. For example, the visit of a theatre-in-education (TIE) company, or forum theatre practitioners with pre-performance and follow-up programmes of participatory work.

■ As a methodology to generate enquiry work across the curriculum through the mantle of the expert, a cross-curricular dramatic-enquiry approach to teaching and learning or through a series of process drama lessons

■ Visits by pupils to museums, galleries and theatres and follow-up programmes of work, which may include re-enactments and re-interpretations of plays and exhibitions

Sources and references

Books

Ackroyd, J. and Boulron, J. (2001). *Drama for Five to Eleven Year Olds.* London: David Fulton.

Boal, A. (2002) *Games for Actors and Non-actors.* London: Routledge.

Brizman, D. (2003) *Practice Makes Practice.* New York: Suny Press.

DfID (2005) *Developing the global dimension in the Classroom.* London: DfID.

Dickinson, R. and Neelands, J. (2006) *Improve Your Primary School Through Drama.* Cambridge: CUP.

Elmessiri, N. and Elmissari, A. (1996) *A Land of Stone and Thyme.* London: Quartet.

Fleming, M. (2001) *Teaching Drama in Primary and Secondary Schools.* London: David Fulton.

Fisk, R. (2005) *The Great War for Civilisation.* London: Harper.

Foucault, M. (1980) 'Truth and Power'. In Cordan, C. (eds.) *Power/Knowledge.* New York: Pantheon Books

Freire, P. (1998) *Teachers as Cultural Workers.* Oxford: Westview Press.

Knowles, E and Ridley, W (2006) *Another Spanner in the Works: challenging prejudice and racism in mainly white schools.* Stoke on Trent: Trentham

Neelands, J. (2000) *Structuring Drama Work.* Cambridge: CUP.

Owens, A. and Barber, K. (2001) *Mapping Drama.* Carlisle: Carel Press.

Simms, K. (2003) *Paul Ricoeur.* London: Routledge.

Winston, J. and Tandy, M. (2004) *Beginning Drama 4-11.* London: David Fulton.

Websites

National Drama and Norfolk County Council (2007) *Drama for Learning and Creativity.* http://d4lc.org.uk

National Association for the Teaching of Drama (2008) *NATD Website.* www.natd.net

Essex County Council (2008) *Mantle of the Expert.* www.mantleoftheexpert.com

Chapter 10

Art, Music and the global dimension

Ian McDougall (Art)

Sian Duffty (Music)

Rationale

In Art and Music, children should experience creative processes and means of expression drawn from diverse cultures and traditions. They should begin to appreciate the distinctiveness of approaches and forms, as well as ways in which styles and techniques influence each other in global terms. However, appreciation and experimentation with forms from diverse cultures should be more than just a pick-and-mix approach. Discussion and evaluation should focus on respect for the unfamiliar and an appreciation that some cultural limitations on art and music can inspire, rather than restrict creativity. The interdependence of cultures and the resulting cross-fertilisation of ideas can be explored in many ways – through similarities in rhythms, designs and patterns from different traditions and through the work of professional artists and musicians: mehndi and the ephemeral art of Andy Goldsworthy, the *kora* playing of Toumani Diabaté and the work of harpists from Celtic traditions.

These activities introduce children to products and creative processes drawn from diverse cultures. They also suggest ways in which creative activities can be used to celebrate cultural diversity and express shared ideas and values.

Art
Activity Ideas for Foundation Stage and Key Stage One

Hands around the world

Drawing around a hand and cutting it out is a familiar activity for young children. A range of displays can be made from these single hands, often with a global message. Literally putting the hands around a world map is good or else making a design from them .You could take the opportunity to colour the hands in with skin tone crayons – chunky crayons in a range of colours, reflecting the diversity of human skin. Skin tone crayons are available from many art shops or educational suppliers.

Aboriginal Hands

Staying with the hand theme – a good use of hands is as a stencil, inspired by the rock art of native Australians. Either using children's hands or cut-outs, use a garden hand-spray, to spray around the hands with water based ink. Be sparing and don't try to do too much at once! You can build up large pieces of work using this technique and involve all the children in a setting. Make sure you use earth colours – shades of black, brown and orange – and the end results will be stunning.

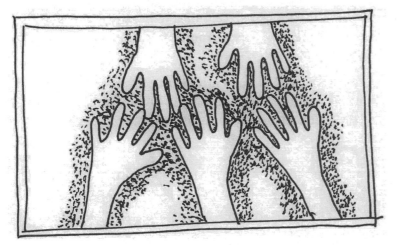

Figure 9: An image inspired by Aboriginal rock art.

Portraits

Several books are available which focus on the appearance and lifestyles of individual children to celebrate cultural and ethnic diversity, alongside shared values, needs and aspirations. They include:

- Damon, Emma (1995) *All Kinds of People: A Lift-the-Flap Book*. London: Tango Books

- Kindersley, Annabel and Kindersley, Barnabas (1995) *Children Just Like Me*. London: Dorling Kindersley

- Kindersley, Annabel and Kindersley, Barnabas (1999) *Millennium Children of Britain: Just Like Me*. London: Dorling Kindersley (now out of print, but still available from some online booksellers)

- Thomas, Pat (2003) *The Skin I'm In*. Hauppauge, New York: Barron's Educational Series

- Zobel-Nolan, Allia and Sakamoto, Miki (2005) *What I Like About Me*. Pleasantville, New York: Reader's Digest

Inspired by shared reading and discussion, children can use mirrors to make self-portraits and make portraits of others, featured in the books. A mixed media approach can be used.

Figure 10: A collage of human faces to celebrate diversity and similarity.

Water Play

Figure 12: Decorated gourds are used as containers and tools in a number of cultures.

Figure 11: A gourd is a hollow, dried shell of a fruit from a family of plants that includes the squash, pumpkin and cucumber.

Gourds are used across the world as carriers and containers. They are also used for musical instruments and jewellery. They are often decorated with wonderful patterns burnt into the skins. Specialist suppliers can provide gourds from a range of cultures and traditions. They make a great resource in a classroom for storage and especially for water play – spoons and jugs from natural materials can provide a distinctive dimension to children's play, contrasting with the plastic and metal containers that are usually available. Patterns and designs on gourds can inspire pattern making, using markers and inks, on other natural materials, such as wood offcuts or pebbles from a beach. Varnishing them can make designs more permanent and give them an added lustre.

Activity Ideas for Key Stage Two

Permanent Markers and water based inks

This starting point can be used over and over again, whenever you are looking at new designs and patterns. You could be looking at cloth or pottery, gourds or prints.

Figure 13: This is a piece of artwork is taken from the design around the edge of a child's skirt, bought in a local market for just a pound or two.

For the design above, the child copied the pattern and picture in pencil and then went over it in permanent marker. After that, she used a limited pallet of inks – don't give too many choices of colour! She inked over the pattern and, of course, the ink did not cover or smudge the permanent marker – it's as simple and as effective as that.

Mehndi designs

Mehndi (or Henna) is the application of henna as a temporary form of skin decoration. It is a traditional, ephemeral art form, from South Asia, North Africa and the Middle East, typically done on special occasions, particularly at weddings. Patterns are usually drawn on the palms and feet. In the class room, the *mehndi* patterns can be created using eye liner, as seen here with two University of Chester student teachers.

Figure 14: Creating mehndi designs

They firstly researched and designed their hand painting on paper, and then transferred it to real skin: eye liner washes off easily. In a classroom the same thing can be done on hands, or else on paper hands cut out especially for the purpose. A stunning display can be made using various traditional patterns.

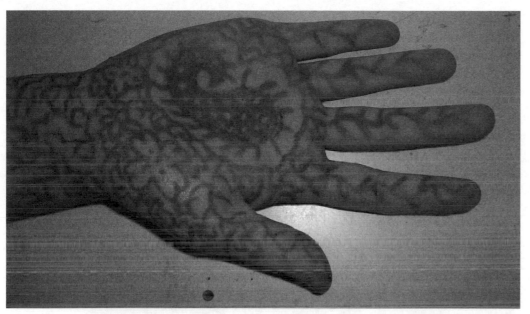

Figure 15: A finished mehndi design

Three-dimensional low relief paper sculptures

This is a great way of presenting children's work and getting them to look carefully at patterns. For this work, the starting point needs to be any patterns taken from cloth, ceramics or traditional artwork from a particular culture. It is best, especially with younger Key Stage Two children, to make copies of the patterns which you would like the children to study. This helps them to focus during the first stage of the work, which is drawing. Give the children an A3 piece of paper and get them to copy the patterns – filling up the whole paper. When they have finished this, they can cut out any shapes that they have created, and then screw up the whole paper at tightly as they can.

Open it up and screw it up again – a time or two! This gives the paper the appearance of a crinkled fabric. Now, carefully rip all the edges off the paper. Open the paper up, take it outside and spray it with black water based ink. Use a garden hand-spray and don't overdo it! Leave it to dry.

In the next session – and you will be surprised how good the pictures look at this stage – you are going to reinforce the edges of the picture with wire. You need garden wire – thick enough to support the paper, but thin enough to bend easily with the hand. Cut two pieces of wire, ten cm or so longer than the long edge of the paper, and lay them on the back of the picture down each long side, with an equal amount of wire overhanging on each side. Using small ripped-up bits of scrap paper and PVA glue fasten down the wire to the back of the pictures and let them dry.

Now comes the artistic part for the teacher/helper: each picture can be joined to the next by twisting the wire together, end to end, thus making a snake of the pictures. Fasten them to a notice board with a staple gun, allowing the snake to stand out from the board.

Figure 16: This group sculpture makes a stunning display which will be particularly effective from a distance

Using pottery to make plaques

Many schools have access to clay and kilns: this is an idea for some pieces of art which will be valued by children and families for many years. Self-hardening clay can be used, but clay fired in a kiln is stronger and lasts longer.

A simple way to deal with clay is to roll it out and make a tile. A non-uniform tile is best – it doesn't really matter what shape it is. To roll clay out you will need a piece of hessian on the table to stop the clay sticking and a wooden rolling pin. Roll out your tile. Then, using other bits of clay, make a low relief picture on the tile. You could also carve into it, making patterns. Don't forget to put some holes in the top of the tile before it dries! If you want, you can bend the tile round while it is still wet – thus making a free standing pot.

The tiles could be inspired by designs, images and patterns from diverse cultures – masks from South East Asia or Mexico, Maori ancestral carvings or Celtic faces. Once dried, the tiles can be painted and glazed.

Figure 17: The design on this tile was based on a piece of cloth from a *sari* length. It contains some of the patterns which the child saw in the cloth. It can hang outside or in and would make a fine garden sculpture.

Decorated homes

Nomadic peoples from around the world have homes which are movable and are decorated with symbols, designs and patterns. Bedouin tents, the tipi of Native Americans, Romany Gypsy wagons or *vardos* and working narrowboats from the English canals are all highly decorated in culturally unique ways. Making models of them can be a celebration of diverse cultures and a way of exploring shared artistic values.

Figure 18: Traditional roses and castles designs on the door of a modern narrowboat

Fig. 19 A highly decorated Romany *vardo*

Following research into the appropriate patterns and designs, models made from stiff paper or card can be decorated with felt tip pens, markers or water-based inks.

Resources for the activities

Aboriginal hands

Stencilled images, produced by Native Australians, occur widely across Australia and some fine examples of stencilled hands are found in the Carnarvon Range in central Queensland. The *Aboriginal Art Online* Website – www.aboriginalartonline.com – contains many images of Aboriginal art, including hands similar to those in Figure 9.

Water play

Decorated gourds from a range of cultures and traditions can be obtained from specialist suppliers, such as *Starbeck Educational Resources* – www.starbeck.com. Alternatively, loan boxes of artefacts from your local Development Education Centre may contain examples.

Mehndi designs

A Web search will give access to a range of sites showing mehndi and henna designs. Some sites may not be suitable for children, so you will need to check their suitability before giving children access. The entry on Wikipedia – http://en.wikipedia.org – is a clear, accurate summary.

Decorated homes

Coppock, Lilian (2003) *Art of Different Cultures.* London: Belair

This excellent book in Belair's series on display in primary schools provides inspiration for all the activities, but specifically gives instructions on making a model tipi and a Gypsy vardo.

Pickford, B and Pickford, T (2006) *Appleby and its fair: A contrasting locality photo pack for Key Stage Two.* Chester: Cheshire County Council

As well as giving background information and providing activity ideas on Gypsy/Traveller culture and lifestyles, this pack contains a template for a model vardo and sample decorative designs.

Young, Ann (2003) *Paint Roses and Castles: Traditional Narrow Boat Painting for Homes and Boats.* Newton Abbott: David and Charles

Background information and practical guidance on narrowboat decoration, with lots of examples.

Music
Background to Activities

Music happens to be an art form that transcends language (Herbie Hancock)

Music is truly global; something that forms an integral part of diverse cultures around the world, whether written for its own sake or in response to emotions, events or the natural world. As Victor Hugo put it: 'Music expresses that which cannot be said or which is impossible to be silent.' Children and adults alike are surrounded by music. We should enable children to listen to the vast range of styles of music that the world has to offer, appreciate the cultural traditions they represent and develop the musical knowledge that can be gained from an appreciation of this range. Singing is one enjoyable way of learning about cultures, the history of peoples around the world, their varied styles of music and, at the same time, developing musical knowledge, understanding and appreciation.

The activities described below are starting points from which you may develop your own ideas. They allow children to listen to music from around the world, to respond to it, to appraise what they hear and to compose. The global dimension is integral to music in the National Curriculum – Programme of Study Key Stage One 5d requires that children experience 'a range of live and recorded music from different times and cultures' and for Key Stage Two 5e, 'a range of live and recorded music from different times and cultures'.

NB: If you use any music from the Web, ensure that it is downloaded appropriately and paid for.

Activities for Key Stage One
Listening to music from around the world

If you use the QCA scheme and the geography unit relating to Barnaby Bear, you could use Barnaby and his travels as a simple way to introduce children to the music of other cultures, as well as to the geographical features of other places. Extracts should be kept quite short and encourage children to express their thoughts about what they hear using the musical elements.

Resources

- QCA Geography scheme of work Unit 5 *Where in the World is Barnaby Bear* – available at www.standards.dfes.gov.uk/schemes2/geography/geo5

Websites, providing access to music from diverse cultures, include:

- *Putamayo Kids* – www.putumayo.com/en/putumayo_kids.php – is a global music label, which has a good selection of CDs with songs and music from around the world, including Brazil, France, Asia, the Caribbean and Africa.
- *The National Geographic Music Website* – http://worldmusic.nationalgeographic.com – has a fantastic range of music from around the world, available to listen to and purchase specific tracks.

Lullabies

Traditionally, music has been used to soothe young children to sleep in the form of lullabies. With the youngest children, you could start with stories such as, *Can't you sleep Little Bear* (see Resources), for example, and talk to the children about why the bear can't sleep and what might help him to get to sleep. Ask them what helps them get to sleep. Do any of the family sing to them to help them get to sleep at bedtime? This will lead into songs the children have heard and are familiar with, for example, *Rock-a-bye, baby*. You may find the song with slightly different lyrics in several songbooks, for example, in the songbook *Sing Hey Diddle Diddle* (see Resources), the song is titled *Hush-a-bye, baby*.

Lullabies are a feature of all musical traditions and several Websites (see Resources) provide examples of lullabies from Europe, North America, Africa and Asia. Get the children to listen to some familiar and less familiar lullabies. As lullabies are usually simple and repetitive, regardless of the language in which they are sung, children can join in and also respond with movement. For each lullaby, discuss with the children how it makes them feel? Why does it do that? What is it about the music? Is it fast, slow, quiet or loud? This will get the children thinking about the musical elements and how they are used for effect in a lullaby.

Resources

- Harrop, Beatrice and Sebba, Jane (ed.) (2001) *Sing Hey Diddle Diddle: 66 Nursery Songs with Their Traditional Tunes* (with Audio CD). London: A & C Black
- Waddell, Martin (2003) *Can't you sleep, Little Bear?* London: Walker Books

The following Websites give useful background information about lullabies and nursery rhymes, including downloads:

- Nursery Rhymes – Lyrics and Origins – www.rhymes.org.uk
- Lullabies from the Cradle – http://lullabiesofeurope.wetpaint.com
- Mama Lisa house of English Nursery Rhymes – www.mamalisa.com/house
- Songs for Teaching: Lullabies – www.songsforteaching.com/lullabies
- Sara Jordan's Lullabies Around the World – www.sara-jordan.com/product-115.shtml
- BBC Radio 3 World Music – World on Your Street: Lullabies from around the world to listen to – www.bbc.co.uk/radio3/world/onyourstreet/chlullaby1.shtml

Activities for Key Stage Two
Stringed instruments around the world

The initial session may be started through discussion. Open the discussion by focusing on the instruments the children know which use strings – for example, guitar, violin or banjo. Some children may already be playing a musical instrument so it is useful to draw on their knowledge and experience

For the first lesson you may decide to focus upon the guitar. Have a guitar in the classroom for the children to look at and explain the various parts. Encourage the children to talk about how it is played. Engage the children in listening to the sounds that can be made on the guitar: plucking, strumming, moving fingers up and down the frets and how the pitch changes. What is the function of the sound box? If you play the guitar yourself, allow the children to listen to the sound of the guitar and encourage them to describe the sound they hear (timbre). You could also listen to CD recordings of guitar music.

To engage with the global dimension, you could go on to look at similar instruments around the world – does the guitar feature in any other countries? What are the origins of the guitar?

You may then want to focus on a particular country or culture and investigate the stringed instruments played. Looking at the stringed instruments of Greece would make an interesting comparison, where children could look for similarities and differences between the classical guitar and those instruments from Greece such as the *bouzouki*. This type of activity could engage some interesting comparative language as well as develop children's understanding of the instruments. Allow the children to listen to traditional music of the bouzouki. There are many CDs available. Can the children compare and contrast the sounds they hear. Is the timbre the same or different to that of the guitar? How is it different? Do other countries have bouzoukis amongst their range of musical instruments? The children will be developing their listening skills as well as appreciating the instruments associated with countries and cultures. Another interesting comparison would be with African stringed instruments, such as the *kora* – a harp unique to West Africa with 21 strings, made famous by Toumani Diabaté, from Mali.

Other lessons could go on to discuss the music of the violin, the drums, percussion instruments in general and the uses of natural materials to create instruments.

Resources
Websites about stringed instruments, include:

- *Traditional stringed instruments of Greece* – http://www.helleniccomserve.com/stringintruments.html – giving background information about the bouzouki and other Greek instruments.
- *All about the kora* – www.soundjunction.org/Allaboutthekora.aspa – gives detailed information about the kora; how it is made and played.
- *World Circuit* is a record label devoted to global or world music. The section of the *World Circuit* Website devoted to Toumani Diabaté includes streamed music from three diverse albums of kora music – www.worldcircuit.co.uk/#Toumani_Diabate
- The *sitar* is a stringed instrument from India and Ravi Shankar is its most famous exponent – www.ravishankar.org

Composing a lullaby
Looking again at the theme of lullabies, children can begin by listening to some of the music composed by the composers of classical music. Brahms's Cradle Song is a good starting point. They can also be introduced to the musical term berceuse, which is French for lullaby.

Using some of the Web links (See Resources for *Lullabies*), you can access a wide variety of lullabies from around the world for the children to listen to and join in; some also have the score and lyrics. Allow the children to listen to a selection of these, possibly two to start with. Once they have listened to each one several times, take their comments and encourage them to appraise what they have heard. You can then start asking questions about their qualities: Why was each lullaby successful? Does it make them want to move, sway? How does it make them feel? You can then start relating questions to the musical elements – dynamics, timbre, pitch, structure, texture, tempo and duration. Are the lullabies characterised by long notes or short notes? Is the pitch low or high? What are the dynamics – quiet or loud? Why one and not the other? What is the tempo – fast or slow? Why? Can they identify the pulse in each lullaby; can they follow it by tapping quietly?

You could go on to create the words for a class lullaby as part of a literacy lesson, which the children can then use as a starting point for their own compositions. Children can compose in small groups. Using their understanding of the musical elements and how they are used in a lullaby, the children can use tuned instruments, voices or keyboards to compose their own lullaby. Alternatively the children start by exploring and experimenting with tuned percussion and keyboards to compose their lullaby – this opens up many creative possibilities.

Resources
Useful CDs include:

- *The Best of Brahms* (Naxos)
- *Berceuse – Music of Peace and Calm* (Naxos)
- *Ninna Nanna: Lullabies (1500-2002) (Alia Vox Spain)*

Pan Pipes

Begin by discussing how a range of instruments are played – blowing, plucking, striking. Focus on blown instruments and get children to identify all the blown instruments they know. Do they know any from around the world?

Introduce the pan pipes and identify their origin in the Andes Mountains of Bolivia, Peru, and Ecuador: if you have a set, show them to the children, discuss what they are made of and invite the children to think of reasons why they are made of the materials they are. Children can be set the task of researching the history of the instrument for homework.

Listen to some traditional pan pipe music (See Resources). Once the children have had chance to listen to the music, discuss with them its characteristics, using the musical elements: dynamics, duration, tempo, texture, pitch, timbre and structure. Can they follow the beat of the music by clapping or tapping?

We have all blown over the tops of bottles to make sounds but have the children tried to make their own pan pipes? Children can create their own sets of pan pipes using plastic tubing (See Resources). Once they have made their pan pipes, they can compose a short piece independently or with others, adding percussion as they go. You may want them to notate their compositions: this can lead to some lengthy discussions about how to go about this. Allow the children to be creative. Compositions will then need to be listened to and appraised. The children can be encouraged to listen for specific aspects of the musical elements – the tempo, the dynamics, the duration of notes – long and short.

Resources

■ A useful CD is *Rough Guide to the Music of Bolivia* (World Music Network)

Websites giving instructions on how to make panpipes, include:

■ *PhilTulga – Music through the Curriculum: Panpipes* – www.philtulga.com/Panpipes.html – gives complete instructions on how to make a set of panpipes from plastic tubing and you can even play a virtual set on the Website.

■ *TeacherVision* – www.teachervision.fen.com – has printable instructions for making panpipes. On the Homepage, click the Printables tab.

■ *Wild Music* also provides clear instructions – www.wildmusic.org/en/aboutsound/soundactivities/panpipes.htm

Food and water

As part of your work on the global dimension you may look at those countries and communities where food is not always readily available, where famine strikes as a result of poor harvests and clean water supplies are scarce. Alternatively, you may want to focus on the food that is wasted on a day to day basis in western societies. For each of these themes there are songs you can to teach the children from the vast range of songbooks that are available on the market. Or you could use the themes as inspiration for children's compositions; creating songs or raps with lyrics that express their concerns and opinions. The rhythms and dynamics of rap music are particularly appropriate for issue-based compositions, enabling children to communicate clear and direct messages to an audience. Children could work in groups, with participants taking on specific roles in the music-making process.

Key questions would include: What are the characteristics of the message they want to convey? Does it need loud music, quiet, fast, slow? Children can then select a few short lines that express their thoughts and use tuned percussion to set their thoughts to music; a truly creative process. You can then encourage the class to listen to each group's songs and comment upon the use of rhythm, pitch, tempo, lyrics and how percussion was used: did it add to or detract from the song?

Physical Education and the global dimension

Luke Jones and Steven Tones

Movement, whether intrinsic or directed, is vital to the balanced development of all children from their earliest years. Physical education as a subject is concerned with developing movement ability in general and in specific ways through activities such as gymnastics, games, dance, swimming, outdoor adventure activities and athletics. Physical Education promotes physical skills and physical development, knowledge of the body in action and positive attitudes to engagement in physical activity. It involves experiencing, learning about and learning through physical activity in a range of areas which require different ways of thinking, selecting and applying skills. Physical Education offers opportunities for pupils to be creative and develop their own ideas, to compete against themselves and others individually and in teams and to face up to and overcome, a variety of challenges in a range of physical contexts and environments.

From a global dimension perspective we believe that PE has the potential to address some of the global challenges by: promoting physical activity for all to advance healthy living; enhancing harmonious active problem solving through collaborative and cooperative working; promoting physical activity as a right for all children; fostering effective social skills such as literacy, communication and fair play.

The global importance attached to Physical Education was underlined when in November 2006, at the 61st Session of the United Nations General Assembly, resolution 61/10 was adopted which acknowledged that:

Sport and physical education can present opportunities for solidarity and cooperation in order to promote tolerance, a culture of peace, social and gender equality, adequate response to the special needs of persons with disabilities, intercultural dialogue, social cohesion and harmony. (Beutler, 2008)

The learning activities chosen for this chapter give children the opportunity to: work together in collaborative, cooperative and competitive learning situations; enhance their literacy skills by describing and explaining the learning activities they are involved in; build resilience to learning and solving problems by reflecting on the decisions they made during and after the lessons; become involved in healthy outdoor learning.

The PE activities are based around outdoor games and include fundamental movements such as run, jump, hop, skip, throw, catch, kick. They include activities drawn from National Curriculum games, athletics and outdoor adventure activities. All the activities can be taught on a school playground or field. By adapting the size of the playing area, the number of participants, the type of equipment and the complexity of the task (ie starting with cooperative games before competitive) all activities can used with children throughout the primary age range.

One starting point (Activity 1) for this work is for children in your class to identify the PE and sport activities that they do both in and out of school and then begin to explore what other children do. If your school is in partnership with a school in a different country it may be possible for children to find out what activities and sports are they have in common. Playground games (Activity 2) allow children the opportunity to work in small groups to design and develop simple games that can be played as part of a formal PE lesson or during break times. Part of the intention is for children to record and swap their games. Activities 3-5 follow more formal approaches to the teaching of games with children being taught basic fundamental games-play and movements through net, target and strike/field games activities. Problem solving activities (Activity 6) provide a great opportunity to have fun and develop co-operative, team work skills in a safe environment that encourages the group to take responsibility for decision making and their own actions.

References

Bailey, R. and Doherty, J. (2003) *Supporting physical development and physical education in the early years.* Buckingham: Open University Press.

Beutler, I (2008) Sport serving development and peace. Achieving the goals of the United Nations through sport. *Sport in Society*, Vol 11, No 4. Oxfordshire: Routledge.

Capel, S. (2005) *Learning to teach Physical Education in the secondary school: A companion to the school experience.* London: Routledge Falmer.

Department of Education (2000) *Fundamental Motor Skill: A manual for classroom teachers.* Melbourne: Department of Education.

Doherty, J. and Brennan, P. (2007) *Physical Education and Development 3-11.* London: Routledge.

Pickup, I. (2007) *Teaching physical education in the primary school: a developmental approach.* New York: Continuum

Pickup, I, Price, L, Shaughnessy, J, Spence, J. and Trace, M. (2008). *Learning to teach primary physical education.* Exeter: Learning Matters

Activity 1: Physical Education and sports

Objectives Learning *By the end of the activity pupils*	Content	Resources	Assessment for *Can a pupil ... ?*
Write a short profile of the Physical Education and sport activities that they are involved in. Find out about the Physical Education and sports activities of children in a school in a different country.	**Learning Task 1** Read Sarah's profile *I walk to school with my brother; it takes us ten minutes or seven minutes if we walk very fast. I have two Physical Education lessons each week with Miss Melonie. In the summer we play games like kwik cricket, football and netball. In the winter, we go swimming and dance in the hall. I like swimming and have my 400m badge. I have been on a school visit to the Conway Centre in Wales where we worked in small groups doing problem solving activities, canoeing, climbing and abseiling. After school I play football for a team in Chester our shirts are blue and white hoops. I've already scored five goals.* **Learning Task 2** In a group of four or five write down on a big piece of paper what Physical Education and sport activities you all do. Ask the teacher to pin the paper to the wall, read what activities other people in your class do. **Learning Task 3** Is your school in partnership with another school in a different country? Find out what Physical Education and sport activities the children do or With the support of a teacher helper use the Web to find out what Physical Education and sport activities children in another country do. **Question**: Do children in Finland ski to school?	Web site – Through Children's Eyes – is a virtual school of cultural exchange carried out between Bufuka Primary School and Kyabahinga School (Kabale District, Uganda) and schools from Turka and Hameenlinna (Finland). It records the activities, sports and hobbies of the children at the different schools.	Write a short profile about their Physical Education and sport activities. Research and find out about the Physical Education and sport activities of children in another school in a different country.

Activity 2: Playground Games

Objectives Learning	Content	Resources	Assessment for
By the end of the activity pupils			*Can a pupil ... ?*
Design and play a playground game with simple rules and structure. Share their ideas with another group of children	**Learning Task 1** Introduce the idea of playing and designing games in small groups on the playground. Read the story *'Harry, Hattie and King Happy Heart'* by Rachel Howcroft, Jai Stark and Caroline Barlow. **Learning Task 2** Provide basic playground games equipment (hoops, bean bags, quoits, skittles, balls etc) for pupils to play with in small groups. Ask children to devise and refine their own playground games. Teacher helpers can work alongside children in discussing their ideas, helping them with brief recording of these and taking photographs of the work/games that are going on. **Learning Task 3** Back in the classroom, ask children in their groups to produce a games card which identifies: the name of their game; the equipment needed to play; the number of players that were required and a list of instructions on how to play the game. **Learning Task 4** Ask children to share their game with another group and or add it to a school Web site page of games and activities played at our school. *Ideas from Scartho Infants School, Grimsby*	**Resources** **Web sites:** *Playground Fun.* www.playgroundfun.org.uk Playground Fun is a website aimed at getting children outside playing games. *Youth Sport Trust.* www.youthsporttrust.org Web site to assist in developing your playground as a learning environment *QCA Physical Education.* www.qca.org.uk/pess Playground activities to improve co-operation and collaboration and raising activity levels.	Work in a small group and contribute to the design and play of a game using simple playground equipment Record by describing their playground game for other children to use

Activity 3: Fundamental skills games (Net games)

Objectives Learning	Content	Resources	Assessment for
By the end of the activity pupils			*Can a pupil ... ?*
1. To explore and use the skill of catching. Eyes on ball, hands provide a target, control with hands only, elbows bend to absorb pass 2. Work co-operatively with a partner to create and play simple net games. 3. Select simple tactics to outwit an opponent in a 1v1 net game.	**Warm up** – Traffic light game. Get pupils to follow instructions: Green – go, Amber – jog on the spot, Red – stop. Develop by adding gears (1-5) for speed of movement (Show what walking quickly at '5' looks like first and emphasise safety – 'no crashes') **Development** – bean bag per pupil for low two handed throw and catch. Challenge pupils to clap, turn around or touch floor before catching; ask pupils for more challenges **Game Play** 1. Sending the bean bag into partner's hoop the other side of a line or net Co-operative play – best collective score after 3 throws each. Competitive play – first to score five times. 2. Can pupils develop their own basic net and wall games with the equipment provided? 3. Introduce competitive 1v1 game which uses two hoops as targets. Pupils can defend by catching the bean bag in flight and attack by using deception or basic tactic of moving an opponent. **Cool down** Moving, throwing and catching. In pairs get pupils to move around the area while passing a bean bag between them. Start at a jogging pace and slow to a walk for the last minute.	Outline a safe area for whole group activity by using cones. Bean bag per pupil for development. Hoop (or similar) and bean bag per pupil for game play.	1. Consistently catch an accurately thrown bean bag with two hands. 2. Work with a partner to create a simple game? *How does it start and finish? How do you score? What are the rules? What if a player breaks a rule?* 3. Understand how to score and win a point and devise a simple tactic to outwit an opponent. *How do you score a point? How can you score a point if a defender is standing in front of you?*

Activity 4: Fundamental skills games (Target games)

Objectives Learning	Content	Resources	Assessment for
By the end of the activity pupils			*Can a pupil ... ?*
1. To explore and use the skill of over arm throwing – Ready (Eyes focused on target, stand side on), aim (throwing arm straight behind body), fire (follow through to target). 2. To choose and use skills effectively for throwing to a target (either over arm or under arm, based on distance from target) 3. Provide verbal feedback to partner on their throwing technique	**Warm up** – Bean game. Ask the pupils to follow instructions: Runner bean – jog in space Jumping bean – jump in space Broad bean – move in wide shape String bean – move in long thin shape Get pupils to devise and demonstrate their own actions for 'Jelly bean', 'Chilli bean', 'Baked bean on toast' ... **Development** – in pairs get pupils to experiment with different ways of throwing to each other. All pairs take a turn to demonstrate one method, which the other pupils try to remember and repeat. Introduce teaching points for the over arm throw (ready, aim, fire) – pupils to practice and give feedback to each other **Games play** 1: Send the bean bag into a hoop – use big hoops as targets; moving further away when successful 2: Bean bag golf. Send the bean bag into hoops distributed around the play ground. How many throws needed to complete a round? **Cool down** – 'Simon says' – to lead pupils through equipment collection, jog, walk, shake, swing, sit for question and answer.	Outline a safe area for whole group activity by using cones. A ball or bean bag (different sizes/shapes) between two for development. (a shuttlecock can be used for introducing over arm throw) Hoop between two pupils	1. Follow two or three simple teaching points to develop a correct over arm throwing action? 2. Understand when different throwing actions are to be used? *Which action allows you to throw for greatest distance / accuracy?* 3. Discuss the tasks set and evaluate others work in relation to simple teaching points.

Activity 5 Fundamental skills games

Objectives Learning	Content	Resources	Assessment for
By the end of the activity pupils			Can a pupil ... ?
1. Value the worth of rules as a means of ensuring fair play.	**Warm up** – Domes and dishes – all cones out, the pupils play one team against the other. One team aims to turn all cones over to a dome, while opposing team aims to turn cones to a dish. Emphasise fair play as pupils will get excited and be tempted to cheat. Ask pupils to devise rules which help to control the game.	Outline a safe working space for a whole group activity and place several cones out in this area.	1. Show that they appreciate fair play in games by following simple rules in a competitive situation.
2. To explore and use the skill of over arm throwing in a simple fielding game – Ready (Eyes focused on target, stand side on), aim (throwing arm straight behind body), fire (follow through to target).		Bean bag between two for throw catch development.	
3. Co-operate with other pupils in playing and scoring a simple fielding game.	**Development** – Paired bean bag throw catch. Stand opposite a partner for continuous throw catch practice. Use this to recap on prior learning. Then encourage pairs to step away from each other every time a bean bag is successfully caught and to step towards each other if bean bag is dropped.	Hoop and bean bag per pair for games play. Hoop, bean bag and four cones for games play.	2. Use an over arm technique to throw for greater distance in a simple fielding game.
	Practice		3. Discuss the fielding games with other pupils, to show that they understand rules and can keep score.
	1: Work in pairs, One stands in a hoop and throws the bean bag down a marked channel. Aim is to move in and out of the hoop as many times as possible before partner returns with bean bag. (introduces the idea of scoring runs)		
	2: In small groups (4s) to play throw rounders. One pupil (the 'batter') starts and throws three bean bags into the game area. On throwing the third bean bag the batter runs around 1st, 2nd, 3rd and 4th base, scoring a point for each one passed. The fielding team can only move once the last bean bag is thrown and aim to stop the scoring of points by returning all three bean bags to a hoop – safely placed by the side of last base.		

Activity 5 Fundamental skills games (continued)

Objectives Learning *By the end of the activity pupils*	Content	Resources	Assessment for *Can a pupil ... ?*
	Everyone has a turn to try to beat own score. (This game can develop in future lessons, with the introduction of a bat – for striking a ball off a tee, bounce feed or from a bowler) **Cool down** return to area with all cones out – get pupils to walk to as many cones as possible in a given time. After repeating the game, get all pupils collect a cone, place in box and sit down.		

Activity 6: Problem Solving

Objectives Learning	Content	Resources	Assessment for
By the end of the activity pupils			*Can a pupil ... ?*
1 Develop problem solving skills based on speaking and listening. 2 Work effectively as part of a team. 3 Evaluate their own and others work effectively.	**Warm up** – Counter balancing. Get pupils to work In open spaces: Can you counter-balance with a partner? How many different methods can you use? Can you counter-balance with a different partner? Can you counter-balance as a group? How many of the group can counter balance at the same time? **Team Challenges** 1 Human Knot – Working as a team, stand in a circle and put all hands in the centre. Hold the hands of two different group members opposite you. You will now have created a 'knot'. Untie the knot, without letting go of hands. You should be able to make 1 big circle – all holding hands. 2 Suspension Bridge – Children to make a chain as far across the space as possible holding hands only. Now put down a marker as a challenge. Can they reach this marker when not limited to only holding hands – they must hold on the next person and not be lying down. 3 Stepping Stones – Work with three flat circle markers only. All of team have to cross the river (width of the hall) by only stepping on the markers. No-one is allowed to touch the floor and the markers cannot be thrown at any time.	Outline a safe area for whole group and team activities by using cones. (Use the warm up to create teams for the following challenges) Shuttle launch will require a large selection of equipment from which children can chose the most suitable for the task.	1 Explore and develop ideas through group discussion and planning. 2 Identify roles and undertake responsibilities for each task. 3 Be able to judge their own ideas and those of others so that they can make decisions about how best to complete the task or challenge

Objectives Learning	Content	Resources	Assessment for
By the end of the activity pupils			*Can a pupil ... ?*
	Team challenge final – Shuttle launch. Based on success in the previous three challenges, teams 'win' the opportunity to collect equipment with which they can build a tower. The aim being to make the tallest possible tower on which a shuttlecock can be balanced. Five minutes total task time in which they have to collect equipment by completing shuttle runs across the hall (1 person at a time, 1 piece of equipment at a time) and build a tower. **Cool down – Bench activity** Children stand on a bench in their teams. Ask them to organise themselves in order of height, shoe size, birthdays, alphabetical order, number of house they live in etc. without touching the ground. Progress to completing the last activity in total silence.		

Chapter 12

The global dimension and Foundation Stage

Chandrika Devarakonda

Rationale

Starting from essentially egocentric perspectives, young children develop ideas about the world from an early age and are influenced by people around them. They are impressionable, active learners who explore similarities and differences with an urgent, open mind. It is the role of Early Years practitioners to provide children with experiences that build trust and establish positive relationships. A global dimension to the Early Years curriculum will provide opportunities for exploring relationships and issues that resonate at personal, local and global levels. The Early Years Foundation Stage curriculum is largely parochial in nature, concerning itself almost exclusively with the development of skills, knowledge and understandings in personal and local contexts. This lack of explicit global contexts should not deter practitioners from including experiences drawn from wider perspectives into their practice. On the contrary, simple and obvious global links can be made throughout the curriculum and the Early Years Foundation Stage expectations, like those of the National Curriculum for later Key Stages, are a minimum requirement not a set of constraints.

It is important for Early Years practitioners to avoid giving young children a view of the world which is coloured by their own perceptions and possible misconceptions. Instead they should look to develop open minds and shared understandings of what it is to be a part of a global, as well as a local community. The starting point for any exploration of the global with young children should be their experience. Within many Early Years settings this may come from the children – experiences from different heritages can be shared and celebrated. Children's holiday experiences may also provide rich source material. In addition to this, the art or food or music of diverse cultures will enrich and enhance experiences. Practitioners should encourage children to make connections: between each other's experiences, between their familiar world and the familiar worlds of others.

There are many activities which could be incorporated into a Foundation Stage setting which support and enhance young children's experience of global connections; below are some examples. The focus should be on developing and extending children's knowledge and understanding of the world in which they live and developing a de-centred concept of themselves as part of a global community.

Resources

Websites

Development Education Association (2008) *Global Dimension Case Studies – Foundation Stage*. www.globaldimension.org.uk/CaseStudies

Learning and Teaching Scotland (LTS) (2007) *Education for Citizenship early years case studies*. www.ltscotland.org.uk/citizenship/sharingpractice

These two web sites provide inspiring case study material for practitioners.

Incorporating the global dimension in the Foundation Stage

Area of Learning	Suggested activities
Personal, social and emotional development	■ The wants and needs of children around the world are as varied as the contexts and circumstances are different. These can be visualised using pictures and photographs, from a range of sources, including: UNICEF (2003) *A life Like Mine*. London: Dorling Kindersley ■ Children listen to stories from different parts of the world, especially those which stress common values, such as what is right and wrong, and attitudes, such as respect for others. ■ Discuss different countries visited as part of holidays, visiting families, or for religious purposes – photos of the children from their holidays could be used to portray different contexts. Encourage children to identify similarities between the different contexts, as well as differences.
Communication, language and literacy	■ Children learn to say some important words in different languages, irrespective of whether there are children speaking different languages in the setting. ■ Share books in different languages, as well as bi or tri-lingual texts
Problem Solving, Reasoning and Numeracy	■ Count using numbers from different languages. ■ Play counting games (hide and seek, for example), using different languages. ■ Sing counting songs in different languages.

Area of Learning	Suggested activities
Knowledge and understanding of the world	■ Invite parents and visiting speakers to contribute to enrich the children's knowledge, skills and attitudes through stories, puppet shows, and artefacts from around the world.
	■ Children discuss food from different parts of the world. Invite parents or extended family to discuss food and how it is eaten. Discuss similarities and differences.
	■ Children explore photographs, books and artefacts from around the world and reflect on similarities and differences between people and places locally and elsewhere in the world.
	■ Children take part in role play (such as being a travel agent) to explore what different places are like using brochures, pictures and children's own holiday photographs; find these places on maps and globes.
Physical development	■ Children play games and learn dances from different cultures.
	■ Raise awareness of children with different physical abilities – athletes, gymnasts, footballers.
	■ Raise awareness of children from other places and how they walk long distances to access water, find food and attend school.
Creative development	■ Encourage children to share their knowledge about music, dance and games from different countries in the world.
	■ Invite parents and visiting speakers to contribute to enrich the children's skills through creative activities using simple materials.
	■ Children use patterns, textiles and designs from diverse cultures and countries in a creative way.

Chapter 13

Global Cross-curricular Theme 1 – Gypsy and Traveller Communities and Culture in Key Stage One

Barbara Pickford

The Traveller Community is composed of a number of different groups:

- Gypsies (English and Welsh)
- Travellers (Irish and Scottish)
- Fairground/Showpeople
- Circus Families
- Boat dwellers
- New Travellers
- Roma – the term used for Gypsies in mainland Europe

The term Traveller is acceptable to most members of these groups, although families from eastern and central Europe usually prefer to be called Roma. The largest proportion of Travellers in schools is from Gypsy and Irish Traveller families. Gypsy and Irish Travellers are ethnic minority communities and are protected by the Race Relations Act 1976 and Race Relations (Amendment) Act 2000 in England and Wales. It is estimated that there are up to 150,000 Travellers across the United Kingdom and, in some areas, they are the largest ethnic minority group. Although Traveller families have lived alongside the settled population for hundreds of years (the first authenticated record in England is in 1514), often little is known about this group of people amongst the non-Traveller community. Travellers are frequently treated with hostility and suspicion and this is not helped by negative images in the popular press. Racism against Travellers is widespread. Trevor Philips, then chair of the Commission for Racial Equality, said that for Gypsies and Travellers, 'Great Britain is like the American Deep South was for black people in the 1950s.'

For centuries it was widely believed that Gypsies came from Egypt, probably because of their dark complexion, hair and colourful, exotic clothing. This is where the name Gypsy comes from – meaning 'Little Egyptian'. Later research however identified that Gypsies in fact originated from north-west India. There are similarities between Gypsy language and culture and the language and culture of this region. Many Travellers speak one of the Travelling languages – Romany, Shelta or Gammon. The majority speak Romany. Teachers have little evidence that Traveller children can speak Romany, but there are still some homes where this is the dominant home speech. Romany was never a pure language as the nomadic tribes which left India probably spoke several languages, such as *Hindi* and *Punjabi*, and as they moved westward along different routes, the groups would have picked up many different root words.

Just as Travellers have no single language, so there is also no single culture. However, there are characteristics which are common to all groups:

- Intense loyalty to the extended family and clan

- Belief in God and the Devil and predestination

- Preparing children in early adolescence to learn the family trade

- Traditional conservative family structures in which wives look after the home and husbands go out to work.

- Rules of hygiene based on ancient Hindu laws, which involve the beliefs that toilets and showers should be situated outside the home to guard against spiritual uncleanliness

- Running water is not used for washing dishes, cleaning teeth and washing clothes. Clean water is poured from closed cans, to prevent contamination. Bowls and utensils used for different purposes are strictly separated

The law is not on the side of people who want to live in caravans and pursue a nomadic lifestyle. Although some Travellers live on well-maintained, well-run privately owned or council run authorised sites, these often occupy bleak locations close to motorways, railway tracks and urban wasteland where no one else would want to live and where they cannot be seen. There is a national shortfall in the number of authorised sites needed to accommodate Travellers and there is currently no statutory duty on local authorities to provide sites. It is believed that more than 30 per cent of the Traveller community have no legal place to stay. Travellers may purchase their own land for sites but usually experience problems in obtaining planning permission.

Many Travellers have had no option other than to camp illegally on unauthorised sites, such as on the roadside, disused factories or car parks where they are vulnerable to eviction at any time. Camping illegally can also cause tension and bring them into conflict with neighbouring communities. Access to health, education and social services can be difficult or impossible for Travellers on unauthorised sites. A recent report, *The Road Ahead: Final report of the independent task group on site provision and enforcement for gypsies and travellers* (2007) concluded that increasing site provision should be a top priority for central government, regional assemblies and local authorities and that the scale of the problem was actually quite small with only the equivalent of less than one square mile of land being needed across England.

As a result of the shortfall of site provision, the majority of Travellers live in conventional houses. Many, however, view housing as a last resort, as they then face separation from extended family groups and they can also experience prejudice and discrimination from the local non-Traveller community. Traditionally, Travellers provided mobile workforces of seasonal labour; they were knife and tool grinders, hawkers and traders in horses and homemade goods. However, with increased mechanisation and the increase of manufactured goods and also the expansion of the road networks, they have had to adapt their skills to meet modern needs. Today Travellers' work may include, tarmacing, block paving, fitting UPVC fascias, antique dealing, garden clearances, tree lopping, horse dealing, or scrap collecting. Most of the family will contribute towards earning a living and children become involved from an early age.

Historically, Travellers have tended to shun education for fear of forced assimilation or because it is seen as an instrument of control. Within family communities, schooling is often a low priority and few adults will have had positive experiences of school. There is also a fear that children will be bullied, harassed and discriminated against. In a report by The Children's Society, *This Is Who We Are* (2007) nearly nine out of ten children and young people from a Gypsy background, who were interviewed, had suffered racial abuse. Nearly two-thirds (63%) reported having also been bullied or physically attacked. In their report, 'Raising the Attainment of Minority Ethnic Pupils' (1999), Ofsted found that: '... the level of hostility faced by Gypsy Traveller children is probably greater than for any other minority ethnic group.' Recent initiatives by the Department for Children, Schools and Families (DCSF) seek to address the increasing underachievement of Gypsy, Roma and Traveller (GRT) pupils and the widening of the gap between the attainment of GRT and non-GRT pupils. It is estimated that only 19 per cent of Irish Traveller children and 9.9 per cent of Gypsy children in education achieved 5 A*-C passes at GCSE in 2006 and that nationally over 10,000 Gypsy and Traveller children are not registered with a school (Independent Task Group on Site Provision and Enforcement for Gypsies and Travellers 2007). The DCSF has launched *The Gypsy, Roma and Traveller Achievement Programme* (2008), which is part of National Primary and Secondary Strategies and aims to improve the quality of provision, improve rates of attendance and standards of behaviour and raise attainment for GRT pupils.

Many local authorities in England have Traveller Education Services (TES) who work with schools and the Traveller communities to ensure that they have opportunities for education. Over 90 per cent of local authorities have Gypsies and Travellers either living in their area or passing through. Promoting an understanding and awareness of Traveller culture and lifestyle amongst the educational community and the promotion of community cohesion is high on the priorities of Traveller Education Services. Education about the Traveller community should start in the earliest years of education and should continue throughout children's formative years as part of their systematic and planned curriculum. June 2008 saw the introduction of the very first Gypsy Roma Traveller History Month providing an excellent opportunity to celebrate the rich cultural heritage of the community. This will be repeated in future years.

Homes is a topic that could easily incorporate teaching about Gypsies and Travellers. Many excellent teaching resources have been produced in the past few years, mostly by Traveller Education Services, for the inclusion of teaching about Gypsy, Roma and Traveller children; the majority are reasonably priced. Two resources that could be used in the teaching about Houses and Homes, and would compliment each other well, are a book entitled *Come and Count with Me* and a photopack entitled *Hatching Tan* (2005). These have been produced by Nottinghamshire and Cheshire TES respectively (see Resources).

Come and Count with Me is a tactile counting board book which is available in two sizes, A4 and A5, and has been cleverly made in the shape of a caravan, or trailer as Travellers call their homes. Each double page spread is a photograph of the inside or outside of a trailer and contains a number of objects to find and count and a small piece of material to find and feel. An interactive CDROM is also available. *Come and Count with Me* is popular with both young children and adults and provides an excellent stimulus for many questions to be asked and answered. It also gives an opportunity for non-Travellers to see inside a Traveller home and helps to promote positive images of a Traveller home.

Come and Count with Me and the accompanying CDROM provide an excellent opportunity to incorporate teaching about Travellers into the curriculum. The use of the photopack, *Hatching Tan* provides an even better opportunity for non-Travellers to take a look inside a Traveller home and explore the daily life of a young Traveller boy called Leroy, and his family. As well as providing images, (as printed photographs and on a CDROM) of the inside and outside of a trailer, and of the authorised site where the family live, it contains images of many other types of home: detached, semi-detached, terraced, mobile home (trailer, park home) and apartment. There are also examples of homes built during different periods and using different materials. A topic on homes could be explored using the pack, with the Traveller home included in the many types of permanent homes where people live in the UK.

References and sources

- The Children's Society (2007) *This Is Who We Are.* London: The Children's Society

- Department for Children, Families and Schools (2008) *The Inclusion of Gypsy, Roma and Traveller Children and Young People.* London: DCSF

- Independent Task Group on Site Provision and Enforcement for Gypsies and Travellers (2007) *The Road Ahead: Final Report.* London: Communities and Local Government Publications

- National Association of Teachers of Travellers (2008) *National Association of Teachers of Travellers Website.* www.natt.org.uk

- Nottinghamshire Traveller Education Service (2006) *Come and Count with Me.* Nottingham: Nottinghamshire County Council

- Office for Standards in Education (1999) *Raising the Attainment of Minority Ethnic Pupils.* London: Ofsted

- Pickford, Barbara and Pickford, Tony (2005) *Hatching Tan: A UK contrasting locality photo pack for the teaching of geography at Key Stage One.* Chester: Cheshire County Council

Chapter 14

Global Cross-curricular Theme 2 – the World of Puppetry in Key Stage One

Carole Naylor

Puppetry is a popular form of entertainment in many parts of the world and can be a way of passing effortlessly through cultural and language barriers. In some places the tradition of puppetry has attained the level of a sophisticated art form and provides a setting for the exploration of past conflicts and the reinforcement of traditional values, and is a way of keeping traditional stories and crafts alive. In Java, a highly sophisticated form of entertainment called *Wayang kulit* is a theatrical performance of live actors and sophisticated shadow puppets. Turkish shadow puppetry, called *Karagöz*, was first performed in the 16th century and is still popular. In Mali rod puppets, made from natural materials, are part of traditional celebrations. Puppet performances in Europe have a similarly long tradition, especially in countries such as the Czech Republic, where itinerant puppeteers still perform on the streets. A Dutch version of Punch and Judy, called *Jan Klaasen en Katrijn*, is still performed and the popularity of television puppet shows indicates that puppets spark the imagination of both adults and children.

Ideas and issues relating to the global dimension can be explored using puppetry. By studying how puppets are made in different parts of the world children can begin to appreciate the skill and craftsmanship that is the product of hundreds of years of tradition. In many instances, puppets have been produced by making use of materials which are freely available in the local setting. For example, *Wayang kulit* uses two-dimensional puppets that are stylised exaggerations of the human shape, made of buffalo or goat skin. Children can be encouraged to use what is available to them in the local environment, natural or recycled materials, in order to create something and bring it to life.

In addition to being a form of entertainment, puppets are used to pass on a message, as political satire or for propaganda purposes. In Ethiopia presentations using puppets have been found to be an effective way of demystifying HIV/AIDS and providing health education The anarchic figure of a gay Mr. Punch has been used, by a gay theatre group to promote understanding and acceptance of gay issues.

Puppets can be made to move in different ways and performances can take many different forms. In parts of Java the puppeteer sits on the floor behind a low table on which the puppets perform. The shows last for at least six hours during the night, accompanied by *gamelan* music, with speech and singing to tell the story. In the classroom puppets can form a parade, tell a story, sing, dance or help to explain an idea. They can present different sides of an argument, be a source of information or provide a barrier behind which a reticent child might feel able to express themselves.

Puppets can be made from just about anything. Reclaimed materials are often a good source of inspiration; a broken umbrella can be turned into a bat; an egg box can be changed into a dragon's head, an old sock can become a snake or a worm. Puppets can be huge, needing several people to operate them, or tiny finger puppets. They can be highly realistic or creations taken straight from the imagination. They can be simple stick figures or complex mechanisms needing much skill to bring them to life. The most important point is that a puppet must be capable of some form of movement. It must be possible for the operator to give a puppet life by making it move in some way. Without the potential for movement, a puppet is not a puppet at all but simply a model or a doll.

Puppets in the primary curriculum

Making puppets allows children to explore much of the programme of study for Key Stage One (KS1) Design and Technology. In terms of the development of ideas, and in planning to make their own puppets, children can base their understanding of what will work on existing puppets, looking carefully to find out what materials have been used and how the components have been put together. In the Foundation Stage and Key Stage One, children are often designing on the job rather than planning in detail beforehand. With little experience of how materials behave and how they can be fixed together it is hardly surprising that young children find this necessary. Being able to talk through their ideas with each other and with a more experienced adult will reduce the amount of trial and error involved.

In actually making the puppets, whether from recycled materials, natural materials or items taken from school stock cupboards, children can learn to select items that will suit their needs from the choice available to them. At first they are likely to go for novel materials or those with bright colours and you may well want to limit the choice available to young children and introduce unfamiliar materials in a gradual way. Skills in numeracy will be involved in the making stage, as children will need to ask questions such as 'Is this big enough?', 'How much will I need?' and 'Will this fit?' Eventually they will need to consider the making process as a sequence of events in which one thing must be done before another if the whole is to fit together. Measuring, using both non-standard and standard measures, will be involved plus choosing appropriate tools to cut, shape and fix components together.

Young children are often not particularly keen on examining a finished product to see how it could be improved. Once something is perceived as finished they often want to move on to the next task rather than evaluate something made previously. Exploring existing artefacts such as puppets bought in a shop can encourage them to consider questions such as 'What is it made from?', 'How is it put together?', 'Does it move properly?', 'Is it easy to make it work?' and 'Would it work better if it was made of something else?' Getting into the habit of thinking about artefacts in this way can encourage children to evaluate both their own products, and those made by other children, in a more detached and constructive way.

Using the puppets for activities in the classroom will involve skills in speaking and listening. Children can use puppets to engage in discussion, debate, questioning, explaining and role-play. There are few safety issues in the puppet-making activities described below but whenever children have access to scissors or glue the teacher obviously needs to keep a close watch on what is going on. For the most part the activities make use of readily available materials and simple techniques that children can manage without much adult intervention.

Making simple puppets

The easiest hand puppets to make are those that start with an existing body such as a paper bag, glove, mitten or sock (see Figures 20 and 21). All children need to do with these is add features, hair or whiskers in order to give the puppet some character. Simple puppets like these can be made in an hour or two and are ready for use in bringing a story to life or joining in a song or rhyme.

Socks can also be used to form the body of a snake, worm or dragon; the head can be made from folded card (see Figure 22) or from an egg box. Small egg boxes are useful for this because they are already hinged and so can make a large mouth that opens and closes.

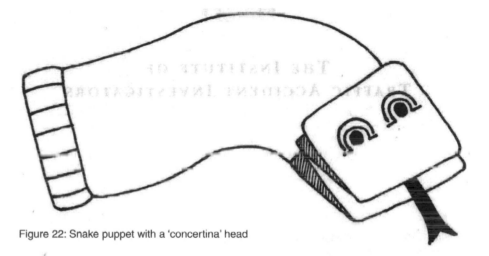

Figure 22: Snake puppet with a 'concertina' head

Finger puppets are easy to make from materials such as felt and can have arms and legs attached (see Figures 23 and 24) to create more movement.

Figure 20: Paper bag puppet; its mouth can be made to open and close with a hand inside

Figure 21: Sock puppet – the hand inside creates movement

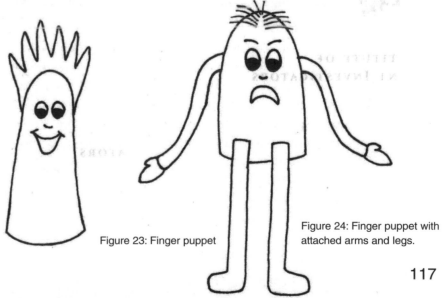

Figure 23: Finger puppet

Figure 24: Finger puppet with attached arms and legs.

117

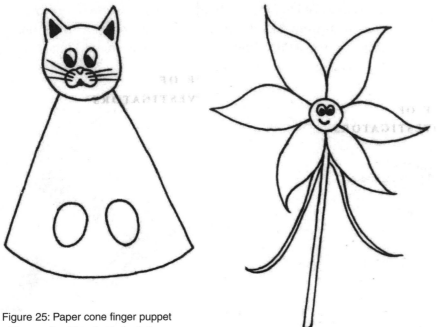

Figure 25: Paper cone finger puppet with an animal head attached; the operator's fingers form the puppet's legs

Figure 26: Simple stick puppet

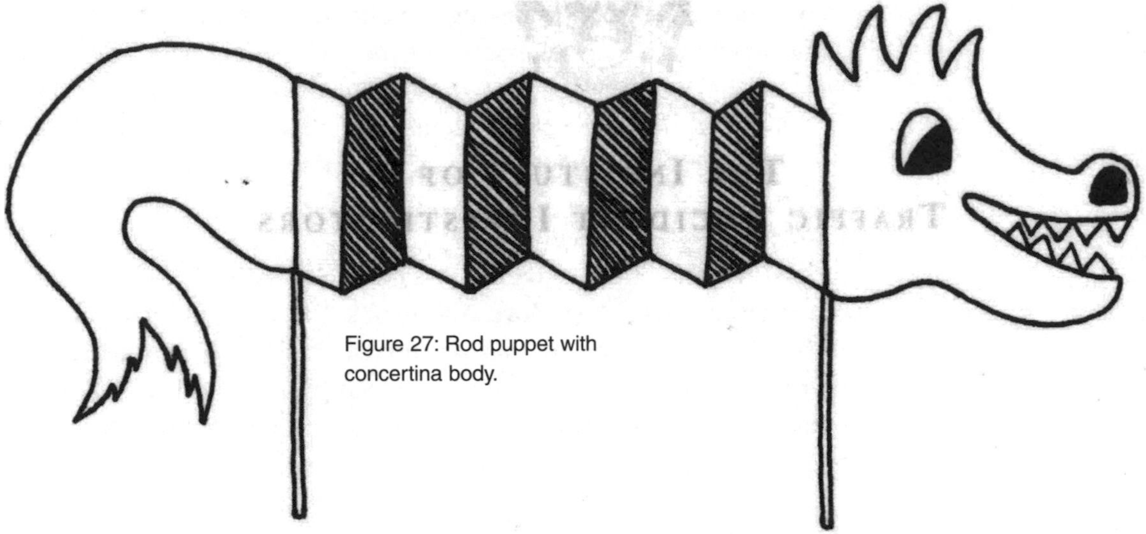

Figure 27: Rod puppet with concertina body.

Card can be used to make flat or cone-shaped puppets that move by children's fingers projecting through holes to form the puppet's legs (see Figure 25).

The simplest stick puppets can be made by attaching a paper plate to the front of a garden cane or piece of dowel; slightly more sophisticated versions of this involve making the puppet's head from card (see Figure 26) and more movement is created with the addition of arms, wings or leaves. Using two sticks to operate a rod puppet allows for more complex creations such as sea creatures, dragons or crocodiles. In the design in Figure 27 movement is achieved by making the body of the creature out of card folded in a concertina style.

Rod or stick puppets made of opaque materials make excellent shadow puppets and it would be good to link this to a topic on light in science as well as comparing children's puppets to images of those used in Wayang kulit. In the past primary children have sometimes made heads for puppets out of papier mache but this is far too long and messy a process to be contemplated by a hard pressed primary teacher. Fortunately it is now possible to buy Model Magic, made by Crayola. This is an excellent material for creating puppet heads for either rod or hand puppets as it is very light in weight and easy to shape; hair, eyes or other features can be poked into it and extra bits attached. When the child is satisfied with his or her design, the head can be left to harden without the need for a kiln.

118

Books as starting points for using puppets to explore themes and issues

Ahlberg, Allan and Ahlberg, Janet (1990) *Starting School.* London: Puffin Picture Books

> Puppets allow children to express their feelings about sensitive issues, with the puppet standing between them and the listener. This story could prompt questions about other schools in other places.

Burningham, John (1999) *Oi! Get off our train.* London: Red Fox Picture Books, Random House

> This is a story to read aloud which explores the plight of endangered animals; animal puppets could be used to enhance the story and allow children to take a more active role.

Dunn, Opal and Winter, Susan (2000) *Acker Backa BOO! Games to Say and Play From Around the World.* London: Francis Lincoln

> Puppets could be used to bring these rhyming and singing games to life.

Gainer, Cindy (1999) *I'm Like You, You're Like Me.* Minneapolis, USA: Free Spirit Publishing Inc.

> Different types of puppets provide a fresh way into exploration of individual similarities and differences.

Souhami, Jessica (1997) *Rama and the Demon King – an ancient tale from India.* London: Frances Lincoln

> Another story to read aloud; puppets can take the part of fantasy creatures – the stranger looking the better! Big book versions of this are available and dual language versions in Punjabi, Gujurati, Urdu or Bengali.

Thomas, Pat and Harker, Lesley (2004) *Conflict: Is it Right to Fight?* London: Hachette Children's Books

> Puppets could be used to explore issues, such as conflict and bullying, raised by this picture book.

WEDG (2006) *Dolls Defying Discrimination.* Canterbury: World Education Development Group

> The book contains ideas for activities using Persona Dolls to explore issues of diversity, discrimination and prejudice; the activities could easily be adapted to use with puppets.

Krebbs, Laurie and Cairns, Julia (2003) *We All Went on Safari – A Counting Journey through Tanzania.* Bath: Barefoot Books

> A story for reading aloud and playing counting games; the animals encountered in the story could take the form of puppets.

Other Resources
Books on puppet making

Butterfield, M (1994) *Making Puppets.* London: Egmont Children's Books

Kennedy, J (2004) *Puppet Mania!* Cincinatti, USA: North Light Books

Llewellyn, C and Spilsbury, L (2005) *Making Puppets.* London: Evans Publishing Group

Martin, L C (2004) *The Art of Recycling.* Massachusetts, USA: Storey Publishing

Tutchell, S Hardy, M Featherstone, S (2003) *The Little Book of Puppet Making.* London: A and C Black Publishers Ltd.

Books on teaching and learning with puppets

Bentley, L (2005) *Puppets at Large: Puppets as Partners in Teaching and Learning in Early Years.* Trowbridge, Wiltshire: Positive Press

Doney, M (2002) *Puppets Around the World.* Danbury, USA: Scholastic Library Publishing

Huff, M J and Barr, M (2000) *Storytelling with Puppets, Props and Playful Tales.* Cambridge: Wizard Books

Shirley-Davies, J and Parkin, J (2005) *Puppets for the Early Years.* Blackburn: Educational Printing Services Ltd.

Crayola Model Magic: around £20 for a large tub (about 1kg.) available from educational and online suppliers.

Chapter 15

Global Cross-curricular Theme 3 – Teaching Climate Change and Renewable Energy Issues at Key Stage Two

Joanne Hurst and Tony Pickford

Rationale

The reports by the Inter-governmental Panel on Climate Change (IPCC) in 2007 removed any doubts that climate change is happening and is the result of human actions. The reports paint a stark picture of resulting environmental damage now and in the future. They identify the urgent need for human adaptation and mitigation measures to be put in place, with the increased use of renewable energy sources being highlighted as a key adaptation strategy, especially in more developed countries. Of these sources, wind energy is a key component and the UK is committed to a substantial increase in the number of onshore and offshore wind farms to meet the target of 20 per cent of electricity being supplied by renewable generation by 2020.

In the context of climate change and the need for greater use of renewable sources, wind energy is a fascinating subject for children to study because it does not offer a simple, uncontroversial solution. Alongside the proponents of wind power in the UK, there is a vociferous lobby of campaigners who doubt its effectiveness as a reliable energy source and deplore the effect on the landscape of wind farms on an industrial scale. Supporters of both points of view come from a green or environmentalist perspective. Groups who agree on most other aspects of sustainable development and have a common concern for protection of the environment, hold vastly different views on wind energy policy – Friends of the Earth and the Campaign to Protect Rural England are good examples.

A thematic study of climate change and renewable energy sources, focusing on wind power, is appropriate for upper Key Stage Two children, developing several key concepts of the global dimension. By evaluating, sometimes conflicting information sources children will develop skills of media literacy, related to the concepts of global citizenship and values and perceptions. Finding possible common ground between different points of view will develop skills of conflict resolution. The concept of sustainable development will be extended by comparing finite and renewable energy sources. Similarly, the idea of Interdependence will be developed by considering the global impact of climate change and the contribution that wind power can make to mitigate its impact.

■ The activities described below are genuinely cross-curricular in that they link to National Curriculum requirements for a range of subjects at Key Stage Two. Activities 1 and 2 address requirements in the science curriculum for children to use 'a range of sources of information and data, including ICT-based sources' for their investigations (Breadth of Study 1c).

■ Activities 3 and 4 have the potential for children to experience a complete designing and making process in the context of design technology, particularly covering the requirement for children to 'assemble, join and combine components and materials accurately' (2d).

■ Activities 5 and 6 link to the geography programme of study through the opportunities for children to 'identify and explain different views that people, including themselves, hold about topical geographical issues' (1d). They will also find out 'how decisions about places and environments affect the future quality of people's lives' (5a).

■ Using a spreadsheet in activity 6 will address elements of the ICT programme of study at Key Stage Two: '... [to] explore models in order to answer 'What if ... ?' questions, to investigate and evaluate the effect of changing values ... ' (2c).

■ All these activities provide opportunities for speaking and listening in the context of literacy in the renewed Primary Framework. Activities 2 and 5, in particular, provide scope for children to debate and discuss, engaging in 'spoken argument, sequencing points logically, defending views with evidence and making use of persuasive language' (Y5 – Speaking). Activities 3 and 4 provide opportunities to develop skills of group discussion and interaction: 'Plan and manage a group task over time using different levels of planning', 'Understand different ways to take the lead and support others in groups' and 'Understand the process of decision making' (Y5 – Group discussion and interaction).

References

■ IPCC (2007) *Climate Change: Synthesis Report – Summary for Policymakers.* Valencia, Spain: IPCC. Retrieved from the Inter-governmental Panel on Climate Change Web site: www.ipcc.ch

■ HM Government (2008) *Energy Bill 2007-08.* HMSO

■ Activity 1 – Climate change

Background

A UK government survey in 2005 discovered that nearly a quarter of children aged 10 to 18 regard climate change as the greatest threat to our planet's future (BBC 2005). Although this implies an understanding of relevant concepts on their part, this is not necessarily the case. The first activity introduces key concepts about climate change, its causes and possible effects. As with most of the activities in this thematic topic, the suggested approach requires the use of an interactive whiteboard or large screen so that web-based resources can be shared with the whole class, supporting explanation, questioning and interactive teaching. This approach meets the needs of auditory and visual learners: the follow-up group activity balances this approach by meeting the more hands-on requirements of tactile/kinaesthetic learners.

Activity

Introduce the key concepts of the Greenhouse Effect and Global Warming using a web-based animation with commentary – a recommended resource is available on the Science Museum Web site (see Resources), although others can be accessed via a Web search, using the search terms: *greenhouse effect animation*. Although the science of climate change requires understanding of some quite sophisticated ideas, it is no more abstract and complex than the principles underpinning the water cycle, a required aspect of the National Curriculum for science at Key Stage Two (Sc2 2e). Reinforce the key ideas and concepts through the use of a group activity involving the matching and sorting of information cards (see *Photocopiables 11 and 12*). In a plenary, use questioning to clarify key points and address any misconceptions.

■ Activity 2 – Renewable energy sources

Background

Having introduced key concepts related to climate change in Activity 1, this activity focuses on the energy sources that are responsible for an increase in greenhouse gases (fossil fuels) and the renewable sources, which may offer more sustainable alternatives. The activity uses enquiry led role-play to provide a focus and audience for research and presentation.

Activity

Using a letter from the chairperson of a local public enquiry into the building of a new electricity generation plant (power station) as a stimulus, give the children the task of finding out the pros and cons of different energy sources in relation to climate change: 'The chairperson wants to know which source of energy to recommend, so that the new plant does not contribute to global warming'. Split the class into groups with the task of producing a short verbal report or to use presentation software such as Microsoft PowerPoint to make the case for and against one energy source. The energy sources that the children research should be a mix of renewable and non-renewable sources such as coal, solar, wind, gas, nuclear and hydro. Several appropriate Web-based sources are available, giving reliable information on energy sources – one of the most accessible is the Children's University of Manchester Web site (see Resources). Get children to report back on their findings in a plenary and hold a class vote on the most appropriate energy source for your locality. Depending on conditions in your area, it is highly likely that wind energy will be one of the more favoured options. Use this to lead into the next activity, which focuses on generation of electricity using a wind turbine.

■ Activity 3 – a wind turbine
Background
Having introduced wind power as a possible source for electricity generation in Activity 2, these activities (3 and 4) focus on the practicalities of wind generation and explore, in miniature, how a wind turbine generates electricity and factors which may influence the efficiency of a turbine. The main activity involves children in making a wind turbine model using design technology skills and resources. Several educational suppliers can provide wood in square-section and strip and dowel forms for the making of a turbine model – see *Photocopiable 14*. Sources for the glue guns, small electric motors, bulbs, voltmeter, data-logger and sensors needed for the task are listed in the Resources section. The description below outlines how children might produce turbine models when given a relatively open design brief. Alternatively, you could provide a detailed design for children to copy – although this limits their creativity, it would allow a more focused fair test, in that the outputs from different sizes of turbine blades could be measured, giving a fair test with fewer variables. The results could then be analysed using a spreadsheet model – see Resources section. Another alternative would be to investigate different materials for the blades such as paper, card, wood, plastic sheet, corriflute.

Activity
Using *Photocopiable 13* or another appropriate image, introduce the features of a wind turbine. Give the children the task of making a model wind turbine, which will generate a measurable amount of electricity. Indicate the resources that are available and get the children to produce a design. Explain that the turbine blades should turn a motor and the amount of electricity produced will be measured by linking the motor to a measuring device: either a voltmeter or a datalogger and voltage sensor. Once designs have been produced, give time and provide resources for children to work in groups to produce their models – the task may occupy several teaching sessions, depending on children's experience and levels of adult support available. Once the models have been constructed have a plenary for the children to feed back on the

issues and problems they encountered in construction. It is likely, if children have been given a relatively free hand in design, that the turbine models will vary in terms of factors, such as height and size of turbine blades. Pose the question: 'How can we make a fair test to find out which turbine produces most electricity?'

An alternative to making a model turbine from scratch could be to assemble a ready-made kit (see Resources), that is suitable for a range of fair tests indoors and out.

Figure 28: Model wind turbine linked to an EasySense datalogger (c)Data Harvest

■ Activity 4 – Testing

Refer back to the question at the end of Activity 3 and draw out from the children the need for a consistent source of wind for a fair test. Suggest a hair dryer or small fan as a source and set up a fair test of the wind turbine designs. Depending on available resources in terms of wind sources, this could be carried out as a whole class activity or by children in groups. The electric motors on each of the models should be connected in turn to a voltmeter or datalogger with voltage sensor. Each turbine should then be subjected to an equal flow of air from a hairdryer or fan for a set time from a set distance – say, a medium wind speed for 10 seconds from a distance of 0.5 metres. The greatest amount of electricity produced (in volts) during the 10 seconds should be recorded. After all the turbine models have been tested, share the results with the class and identify which models produce most electricity. Ask the children to identify possible reasons why some turbines are more efficient than others: depending on the children's designs; factors could include height of model, size/shape of turbine blades and durability of construction.

■ Activity 5 – For and against

Background

After evaluating their turbine models, this activity places the technology in a real world context and explores the pros and cons of wind generation of electricity. Features and issues relating to onshore and offshore wind farms can be explored using the images on *Photocopiable 17*. The suggested extension activity involves analysis of data using ICT. For children, measurement of output from wind farms in kilowatts or megawatts is an abstract notion with little meaning: an indication of the number of homes powered by wind generated electricity is more meaningful. The statistic provided is however merely indicative of the number of homes that a given wind farm might power. In the real world, a huge range of factors will come into play affecting domestic consumption. In the developing world a wind farm is likely to provide power for a greater number of homes than in more developed countries, because of the larger number of electrical appliances in the latter. A wind farm in the UK is likely to provide power for a greater number of homes than the same-sized facility in the southern USA, where domestic air-conditioning equipment is constantly in use.

Activity

To introduce this activity, use a Web-based *Wind Turbine Simulator* (see Resources) to explore the factors which influence wind turbine design in the real world. The simulation should make the point that the most effective turbine design and location is a tall tower in a location with few, if any, buildings. Clusters of turbines or wind farms are therefore most likely to be sited in upland, rural areas. Make the point to the children that many people feel strongly about the appearance of wind farms and their effect on the landscape. Split the class into two groups and give the children the task of finding out the arguments for and against wind farms. Web-based resources (see Resources) could be used or children can be asked to summarise two or three key points from *Photocopiables 15* or *16* about a proposed wind farm in Cumbria. In a plenary, get the two groups to feed back and review the points that are made: – a class vote could be held on the subject. Identify offshore wind farms as offering some solutions to the problems which beset onshore facilities in rural locations. But offshore wind farms also have their detractors, who point to dangers to shipping and possible harm to rare birds as among the problems.

A possible extension activity would be to gather and analyse statistical information about wind farms in the UK and world wide. *Photocopiable 18* provides a possible format for gathering information from relevant Web sites (see Resources) for entering into a simple database program. The software could then be used to answer questions, such as 'Which wind farm in the UK has most turbines?', 'Which country has most wind farms?' or 'Do large wind farms always produce more power than smaller ones?'.

■ Activity 6 – Act local

Background

In this final activity, the focus moves to the children themselves and their families, rather than technological solutions to climate change. The activity focuses on the use of an online carbon calculator and then a spreadsheet model to find out how a household could reduce energy consumption. The spreadsheet model assumes that central heating in the household is not provided by electricity, but by gas or oil or a renewable source: any heaters included in the model are for supplementary heating. Prior to this activity, the children should be encouraged to monitor the amount of electricity usage in their household over a few days.

Activity

Introduce the idea of a carbon calculator as a way of measuring the amount of a greenhouse gas (carbon dioxide – CO_2) produced by a household. Work through the ACT ON CO_2 calculator on the Direct.gov Web site (see Resources) as a whole class activity, using different households as examples. Make the point that household consumption of electricity accounts for a large amount of the CO_2 being produced directly or indirectly by a household through burning fossil fuels in a power station. Introduce a spreadsheet model which enables children to explore 'What if … ?' questions about electricity consumption in a household (see Resources section). Give them a target for reducing emissions, or the household electricity bill, below a certain level, such as halving emissions or the bill. Stress to the children that the only factor that can be changed on the spreadsheet is the amount of time each electrical appliance is used. While children are working with the spreadsheet, prompt them with key questions about the amount of time the appliances are used and which appliances use most electricity. In a plenary, get children to share their results and findings. Conclude by getting the class to consider other ways – apart from the time appliances used – in which electricity consumption and greenhouse gas emissions might be reduced, such as better insulation, wearing warmer clothes indoors and using low energy light bulbs.

Resources

Web-based Teaching Resources

■ Greenhouse Effect animation from the *Science Museum*: http://www.sciencemuseum.org.uk/energy/site/EIZInfogr9.asp or follow the links from the *Science Museum Home page: Science Museum > Online Stuff > Energy – fuelling the future > Energy info Zone > Watch > Greenhouse effect*

■ Energy sources from the *Children's University of Manchester* Web site: www.childrensuniversity.manchester.ac.uk/interactives/science/energy/

■ *Wind Turbine Simulator* from the *Wind with Miller* section of the Danish Wind Industry Association (DWIA) web site: www.windpower.org/en/kids/index.htm

■ ACT ON CO² calculator on the *Direct.gov* Web site: http://actonco2.direct.gov.uk/index.html

Web Resources for and against wind farms

■ *Yes2 Wind* – Web site produced by Friends of the Earth, Greenpeace and WWF, with the aim of providing information and resources for the public to support wind farm proposals locally': www.yes2wind.com

■ *National Wind Power* – from *npower Renewables*: www.natwindpower.co.uk

■ *British Wind Energy Association* – 'Trade and professional body for the UK wind and marine renewables industries': www.bwea.com

Web sites opposing wind farms tend to come and go on the Web as local planning proposals are made and campaigns are set up and wind down – try a Web search, using the search terms 'against wind farm', to find the latest sites. Sites which remain constant, however include

■ Country Guardian – 'A UK conservation group which, since 1991, has campaigned against the construction of wind turbines in environmentally sensitive areas': www.countryguardian.net

■ *Wind-Farm.org*: www.wind-farm.org

■ Campaign to Protect Rural England (CPRE): www.cpre.org.uk

Web Resources about wind farms

■ The Wind Power Wind Turbines and Wind Farms database contains worldwide data plus picture and video galleries: www.thewindpower.net

■ The UK Wind Energy Database (UKWED) is a database on wind energy projects in the UK, both onshore and offshore: www.bwea.com/ukwed/index.asp

Books

Non-fiction, reference books on energy sources and renewable energy include:

■ Bledsoe, K (2004) *Energy Sources*. Perfection Learning

■ Bowden, R (2007) *Energy*. Hodder Wayland

■ Gibson, D (2004) *Wind Power*. Smart Apple Media

■ Green, J (2007) *Saving Energy*. Hodder Wayland

■ Gunkel, D (2006) *Alternative Energy Sources*. Greenhaven Press

■ Morris, N (2008) *Fossil Fuels*. Franklin Watts

■ Morris, N (2008) *Wind Power*. Franklin Watts

■ Stringer, J (2005) *Energy*. Evans

Spreadsheet Resources

The following instructions relate to *Microsoft Excel* spreadsheet software and assume that you have a basic knowledge of spreadsheet terms and functions, including inserting simple formulae and making charts.

Spreadsheet for Activity 3

To explore the effect of different blade lengths on electricity output from a model wind turbine.

Voltage should be measured using a voltmeter or datalogger and voltage sensor attached to an electric motor on the model (see *Photocopiable 4*). A hairdryer or fan should be used to turn the turbine blades.

■ Open a blank *Excel* workbook and enter 'Blade Length (cm)' in cell A1

■ Enter 'Voltage (v)' in cell B

■ In column A enter the blade lengths in centimetres that you wish to investigate – starting with 5 cm and increasing by 2.5 cm intervals, up to around 30 cm (the maximum blade length will be determined by the size of the model)

■ Enter the voltage measurements from the voltage sensor into column B

■ When all the measurements have been entered, highlight the complete table and click on the *Chart Wizard* button in the *Excel* toolbar

■ In the *Chart Wizard*, select a 'scatter graph with data points connected by smoothed lines' and click *Next*

■ In the *Chart Options* window, uncheck the *Show legend* button and label the X axis with 'Blade Length (cm)' and the Y axis with 'Voltage (v)'. Insert a suitable title and click *Finish* to insert the chart into the workbook

It is likely that the resulting chart will look something like this:

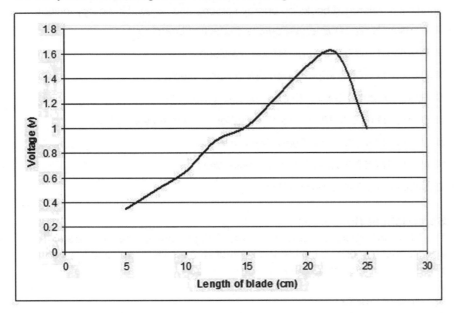

Figure 29 Output from the turbine will increase with blade length, but an optimum size will be reached, after which the weight of the blades is likely to reduce output.

Spreadsheet for Activity 6:
To explore 'What if ... ?' questions about electricity consumption in a household.

18 Open a blank *Excel* workbook and enter Appliance, Power rating (W), Minutes used per day, Units per day (kWh') and Cost per day in cells A1 to E1.

19 List household electrical appliances and power ratings in Watts in columns A and B, as follows:

Appliance	Power rating (W)
Cooker ring	2000
Electric fire (2 bar)	2000
Fan heater	3000
Fridge freezer	150
Immersion heater	3000
Iron	1500
Kettle	2000
Large colour TV	100
Light bulb (e.g. bedside light)	40
Light bulb (e.g. desk lamp)	60
Light bulb (e.g. main light)	100
Oven	3000
Radio	20
Stereo system	75
Toaster	500
Vacuum cleaner	1200
Video recorder	25
Computer	75
Washing machine	3000

Figure 30: Household electrical appliances and power ratings in Watts

20 Enter minutes used in a typical day in column C.

21 In D2, enter the following formula to calculate units per day in Kilowatt Hours (kWh): '=B2/1000*C2/60' and copy the formula down the D column by dragging the fill handle (the cursor shows a black cross).

22 In E1, enter the formula '=D2*B23', where B23 refers to a cell giving the unit cost of electricity, e.g. £0.09 per unit. Copy the formula down the E column by dragging the fill handle (the cursor shows a black cross).

23 At the foot of column D use a SUM formula to add the total units per day (e.g. '=SUM(D2:D20)') and at the foot of column E add the total cost of the appliances (e.g. '=SUM(E2:E20)'). In an adjacent cell, use a formula to calculate the cost per year – multiply the cost per day by 365.

24 Finally, in cells adjacent to main table, calculate carbon emissions for different types of fossil fuel power stations, resulting from the use of electricity in the

household. For each kWh, coal, gas and oil-fired power stations produce approximately 1 kg, 0.4 kg and 0.7 kg of CO^2 respectively. Multiplying these totals by 365 divided by 1000 (eg '=G2*365/1000') will give yearly emissions for CO^2 in tonnes.

Your finished spreadsheet model will look something like this:

Appliance	Power rating (W)	Minutes used per day	Units per day (kWh)	Cost per day		CO2 from Power Station (kg) per day	CO2 from Power Station (t) per year
Cooker ring	2000	30	1.00	£0.09	Coal	56.68	21
Electric fire (2 bar)	2000	360	12.00	£1.08	Gas	22.67	8
Fan heater	3000	120	6.00	£0.54	Oil	39.67	14
Fridge freezer	150	1440	3.60	£0.32			
Immersion heater	3000	240	12.00	£1.08			
Iron	1500	15	0.38	£0.03			
Kettle	2000	45	1.50	£0.14			
Large colour TV	100	360	0.60	£0.05			
Light bulb (e.g. bedside light)	40	120	0.08	£0.01			
Light bulb (e.g. desk lamp)	60	240	0.24	£0.02			
Light bulb (e.g. main light)	100	2520	4.20	£0.38			
Oven	3000	75	3.75	£0.34			
Radio	20	240	0.08	£0.01			
Stereo system	75	180	0.23	£0.02			
Toaster	500	45	0.38	£0.03			
Vacuum cleaner	1200	30	0.60	£0.05			
Video recorder	25	1440	0.00	£0.00			
Computer	75	360	0.45	£0.04			
Washing machine	3000	180	9.00	£0.81			
TOTAL			56.68	£5.10	Per year	£1,861.77	
Cost of electricity per unit	£0.09						

Figure 31: The finished spreadsheet

Design Technology resources

■ Wood in square-section, strip and dowel forms can be obtained from a number of educational suppliers, including TTS (www.tts-group.co.uk) and Technology Supplies Ltd. (www.technologysupplies.co.uk). Glue guns, saws and other tools can be obtained from the same suppliers

■ Technology Supplies Ltd. (www.technologysupplies.co.uk) can supply a simple bench voltmeter, suitable for primary school use

■ Data Harvest (www.data-harvest.co.uk) supply the EasySense datalogger with voltage sensor accessory. They also supply a Wind Energy Kit, comprising 'everything to build a tabletop wind turbine with 12 removable propeller blades, a selection of gears, a bench voltmeter and motor, buzzer and LED'

Photocopiable 11 – Terms and Definitions

Carbon Dioxide (CO_2)	**Renewable energy source**	**Wind turbine**	The effect of the Earth's atmosphere, due to gases, such as CO_2, in trapping heat from the sun	An increase in the near surface temperature of the Earth, caused by the Greenhouse Effect	A place where electricity is generated using an energy source, such as coal or gas
Greenhouse effect	**Climate change**	**Carbon**	A colourless, odourless gas, with the formula CO_2, that is present in the atmosphere. It traps heat from the sun	Fuels (coal, oil, natural gas) that are formed from ancient plant and animal life over millions of years	A machine with large blades which converts wind energy into electrical power
Global warming	**Energy**	**Greenhouse gas**	Fuels that can never be used up. Hydro (water), solar, wind, geothermal and biomass are renewable energy	A term used to describe a change from one climatic condition to another	An element which combines with oxygen to make carbon dioxide (CO_2) and is a basic part of all life on Earth
Fossil fuel	**Power Station**	**Sun**	The ability to do work or the ability to move an objectsources	A gas, such as carbon dioxide (CO_2) or methane, which traps heat from the sun in the atmosphere	The source of all heat and light on Earth

Match each term to a definition.

Photocopiable 12 – The Story of Climate Change

Fossil fuels contain carbon from plants and animals that died millions of years ago	As more carbon dioxide is produced, more heat is trapped in the atmosphere making the Earth warmer and warmer
As the atmosphere of the Earth gets warmer, the weather changes, leading to more periods with little rain (droughts) and more storms	Rising sea levels lead to more floods on the coast
Carbon dioxide is a greenhouse gas that traps heat in the atmosphere	As the atmosphere of the Earth gets warmer, ice melts in the Arctic and Antarctic, making sea levels rise
Greenhouse gases in the atmosphere act like a blanket on the Earth keeping it warm enough for animal and plant life	When fossil fuels are burnt, carbon reacts with oxygen in the air to make carbon dioxide

Try to put the statements in order to tell the story of Climate Change

Photocopiable 13 – A Wind Turbine

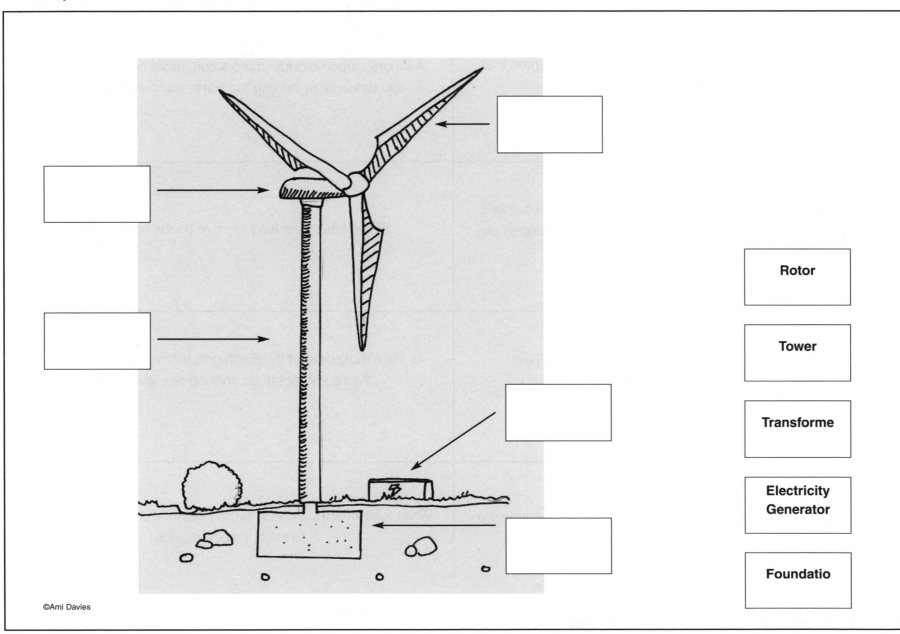

©Ami Davies

Rotor

| Tower |

| Transforme |

| Electricity Generator |

| Foundatio |

Photocopiable 14 – A Model Wind Turbine

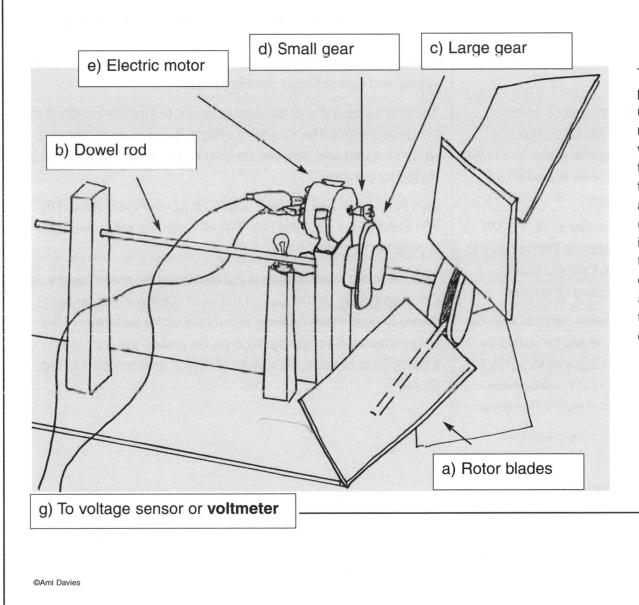

d) Small gear

c) Large gear

e) Electric motor

b) Dowel rod

a) Rotor blades

g) To voltage sensor or **voltmeter**

The **rotor blades**, made from card or plastic, (a) are attached to a wood wheel using short dowel rods. A longer **dowel rod** (b) is attached to the centre of the wheel. The dowel rod is held in place by two upright pieces of wood and can turn freely. A **large gear** (c) on the rod turns a **smaller gear** (d) on the electric motor (e). Wires go from the motor to a **bulb** (f) in a bulb-holder, which lights as the rotor turns the motor and generates an electrical current. Wires from a **voltage sensor** or **voltmeter** (g) are clipped to the motor to measure the electrical current from the motor.

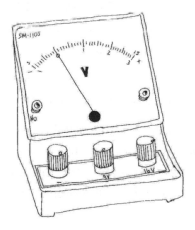

©Ami Davies

Photocopiable 15 – Arguments against the Whinash Wind Farm

The impact, visually, will be immense and destroy beautiful – and largely unspoilt – countryside. It will ruin views from deep within both The Yorkshire Dales National Park and the Lake District National Park.

The valley and fells will be spoiled by the introduction of the scheme. A rare and delicate upland habitat will be completely buried by 5 miles of roadway, with further service roads and huge blocks of concrete needed for turbines. This area is also a bird migration route.

40,000 travellers pass daily through the Lune Gorge on the M6 motorway. For many, this magnificent landscape is the gateway to Cumbria, the highlight of a long journey. The turbines would detract from the natural impact of this impressive landscape.

Distraction caused to drivers on the M6 motorway should also be addressed as an important issue. The scheme will be visible to drivers approaching on the south-bound carriageway for up to 5 miles, and, to a lesser extent, on the north-bound carriageway. On the grounds of safety alone, this scheme should not proceed.

This is a low-flying area for RAF exercises; it may mean the turbines will have to be illuminated.

No scheme of this size has ever been planned in such a populated area and the economic impact will be severe. Tourism is vitally important, with many holidaymakers choosing this area because it is off the beaten track. This type of tourist will certainly be deterred from visiting, to the harm of local businesses including hotels, inns, guest houses, shops, etc. The financial benefit of the Wind Farm enjoyed by a few farmers and landowners will be more than offset by a general loss in property values and tourist-based developments.

There is a possibility of damage to health to those living close to the development. The long-term effects of exposure to different types of sound and possible strobing is not known but must be a matter for concern.

This is Phase 1 of a scheme, which could eventually extend to 150 turbines on adjoining hills. Future schemes will be virtually impossible to stop.

This particular development is not motivated by 'green' issues, but rather by greed. On the part of the wind company, this is the desire to build these turbines regardless of the suitability of the environment whilst making huge profits and on the part of a wealthy landowner, a willingness to exploit a distant part of the Estate.

Based on the Committee Statement from the *Say NO To The Whinash Windfarm* Web site – www.nowhinashwindfarm.co.uk/statement.asp

Photocopiable 16 – Arguments for the Whinash Wind Farm

The proposed wind farm has 27 tall turbines, will produce enough energy for 47,000 homes, cutting carbon dioxide emissions by 178,000 tonnes every year or over 4 million tonnes of carbon dioxide over a 25 year lifespan.

The site is between 1km and 5km from the M6 motorway, which can be seen and heard from much of the site. It lies between the Yorkshire Dales and the Lake District National Park, but is not itself in either National Park. Motorways have been found to have a larger footprint than previously thought and affect wildlife for a large area.

Opponents have used altered photographs showing 41 turbines much taller than those planned and continued to use them long after the proposed number of turbines was reduced.

Cumbria is one of the windiest counties in England, but as it has many protected areas, the sites available for building land based wind farms are limited. Whinash offers a great opportunity for the production of renewable energy and would make a significant contribution to county, regional and national targets.

The latest evidence from climate scientists including those at the recent Hadley Centre conference and the American Association for the Advancement of Science annual meeting, show that there is a need to take every reasonable opportunity to build wind farms.

The reduction of emissions will lessen the chances of damage to the landscape and biodiversity that will be among the most severe effects in Cumbria.

To make the necessary impact on climate change will require action across the planet, but as we have a mere decade to avoid the worst impacts, it is essential that this wind farm is built.

From a Friends of the Earth Press release: *WIND FARM INQUIRY TO TEST CLIMATE CHANGE COMMITMENT –*

www.foe.co.uk/resource/press_releases/wind_farm_inquiry_to_test_13042005.html

Photocopiable 17 – Wind Farms

An onshore wind farm
©Tony Pickford

An offshore wind farm
©Tony Pickford

Photocopiable 18 – Wind Farms Data Gathering Sheet

Example:

Name	Al Koudia
Country	Morocco
Onshore or Offshore?	Onshore
Number of Turbines	84
Total Power Output	50400 kW
Number of Homes	25200

Example:

Name	
Country	
Onshore or Offshore?	
Number of Turbines	
Total Power Output	
Number of Homes	

Name	
Country	
Onshore or Offshore?	
Number of Turbines	
Total Power Output	
Number of Homes	

Name	
Country	
Onshore or Offshore?	
Number of Turbines	
Total Power Output	
Number of Homes	

Name	
Country	
Onshore or Offshore?	
Number of Turbines	
Total Power Output	
Number of Homes	

Name	
Country	
Onshore or Offshore?	
Number of Turbines	
Total Power Output	
Number of Homes	

Note: 1000 Kilowatts (kW) = 1 Megawatt (MW).
1 MW powers approximately 500 homes.

Chapter 16

Next Steps

Alongside those referred to in the subject-focused and thematic chapters in this book, the following resources also provide links, ideas and inspiration for integrating the global dimension into your practice.

Books

Cheshire County Council (2005) *Education for Sustainable Development: A Teacher's Handbook*. Chester: Cheshire County Council

A clear and accessible introduction to this vital concept within the global dimension, with many school-based case studies.

Harrison, D. (2008) *Regardless of Frontiers: children's rights and global learning*. Stoke on Trent: Trentham

Swainston, H and Pickford, T (2005) *Ready Resources: Geography Book 3*. Leamington Spa: Scholastic

This book, supported by resources on CDROM, includes a section on activities to develop ideas about global citizenship and sustainability at Key Stage Two.

Websites

Citizenship Foundation (2008) *Citizenship Foundation Website*. www.citizenshipfoundation. org.uk

An independent UK educational Charity, the Citizenship Foundation promotes citizenship education and provides resources for teaching about diversity and citizenship in a global context.

DEA (2008) *Global Dimension Website*. www.globaldimension.org.uk

Managed by the Development Education Association (DEA) and sponsored by the Department for International Development (DfID), this is the main UK-based Website providing information on curriculum resources relating to the global dimension. All resources, whether from commercial, public or not-for-profit publishers, have been evaluated by a team of Editorial Advisors.

DEA (2008) Development Education Association Website. www.dea.org.uk

Funded by development charities, DfID and Department for Children, Schools and Families (DCSF), the DEA is an educational charity focusing on global learning. The Web site provides links to the 45 local Development Education Centres across the UK, which promote teaching and learning about global issues and 'encourage positive local action for global change' (DEA 2008).

Geographical Association (2008) www.geography.org.uk

The subject association for geography in the UK provides a useful summary of principles and practice in relation to the global dimension in the Teacher Education section of their Website.

Oxfam (2008) Oxfam education. www.oxfam.org.uk/education

The Website of one of the UK's main development charities provides links to published resources and access to *Cool Planet,* a Web site with a range of online activities for children.

Teachers in Development Education (2008) TIDE- Global Learning. www.tidec.org

Provider of resources and training, based in Birmingham.

FALKIRK COUNCIL
LIBRARY SUPPORT
FOR SCHOOLS